Poetry In Motion

West Sussex

Edited by Donna Samworth

 Young**Writers**

First published in Great Britain in 2004 by:
Young Writers
Remus House
Coltsfoot Drive
Peterborough
PE2 9JX
Telephone: 01733 890066
Website: www.youngwriters.co.uk

SB ISBN 1 84460 363 6

Foreword

This year, the Young Writers' 'Poetry In Motion' competition proudly presents a showcase of the best poetic talent selected from over 40,000 up-and-coming writers nationwide.

Young Writers was established in 1991 to promote the reading and writing of poetry within schools and to the youth of today. Our books nurture and inspire confidence in the ability of young writers and provide a snapshot of poems written in schools and at home by budding poets of the future.

The thought effort, imagination and hard work put into each poem impressed us all and the task of selecting poems was a difficult but nevertheless enjoyable experience.

We hope you are as pleased as we are with the final selection and that you and your family continue to be entertained with *Poetry In Motion West Sussex* for many years to come.

Contents

Hazelwick School

Ifield Community College

Adam Hunn (13)	78
Gemma Higgins (14)	78
Eiblisha Taylor & Sharna Evans (13)	79
Shaunie Chisling (13)	79
Joanne Moule (15)	80
James Pearl (14)	80
James Foster (13)	81
Ryan Ellery (12)	81
Stephen Thompson (13)	82
Simone Harris (13)	82

Michael Ayres Junior School
Nicholas O'Leary (10)	83

Millais School
Lana Brooker (12)	84
Sarah Jane Coxall (12)	84
Elspeth Waters Brown (11)	85
Megan Haney (12)	85
Megan Whitty (11)	86
Kelsey Baldock (11)	87
Olivia Barnett (12)	88
Chantal Range (13)	88
Chloe Crellin (11)	89
Kimberley Barker (11)	89
Ella Bussey (11)	90
Chelsea Draisey (11)	90
Hannah Norris (12)	91
Chloe Gladwish (11)	91
Josie Nelder (11)	92
Emily Smith (11)	92
Catrin Williams (11)	93
Rachel Pearson (11)	94
Rachel Banks (12)	94
Charlotte Bearman (12)	95
Jessica Munden (13)	96
Catherine Tingley (11)	96
Gemma McKale (11)	97
Rachael Holding (11)	97
Emma Farnes (11)	98
Lauren Fuller (11)	98

Megan Evans (11)	99
Gemma Rivers (11)	99
Laura Drew (11)	100
Charlotte Perrelle (11)	100
Katie Harding (11)	101
Georgia Gregory (11)	101
Amanda Gilbert (11)	102
Ashleigh Bayton (11)	103
Sarah Kitchen (11)	103
Charlotte Harris (11)	104
Vanessa Robinson Caturla (11)	105
Lara Hutchison (11)	106
Beth Wrigley (11)	107
Lauren Law (11)	108
Francesca Smith (11)	108
Hollie Cousins (11)	109
Mary-Anne Frank (12)	109
Chloe Loader (12)	110
Gemma Humphreys (11)	110
Sophie Goodwin (11)	111
Becky Robins (11)	111
Isobel Darcy (11)	112
Georgina Carr (11)	113
Eleanor Martin (11)	113
Nicola Dexter (11)	114
Molly McLean (11)	114
Katie Hedger (11)	115
Rachel Parker (11)	115
Kristine Bates (11)	116
Rebecca Mash (13)	116
Laura Wallis (11)	117
Lauren Bristow (11)	118
Emma Skelton (12)	119
Ashton Tansey (12)	119
Amy McDonogh (11)	120
Sinead Nugent (12)	120
Charlotte Clark (11)	121
Allana Cheema (13)	122
Clare Munns (12)	122
Stevie Rintoul (12)	123
Amelia Bagwell (11)	123
Georgina Trinder (12)	124

Amy Dimmock (12)   151
Joanne Marychurch (13)   151
Emma Wilson (12)   152
Jade Azhar (12)   152
Rebecca Armstrong (12)   153
Alison Campbell (12)   153
Lorna-Belle Harty (12)   154
Megan Clark (12)   155
Lucy Elkins (12)   156
Martha Allsop (13)   157
April Loft (12)   158

Rydon Community College

Ryan Hunter (11)   158
Rachael Ann Lewis (11)   159
Amy Gooding (11)   159
Amber Leask (12)   160
Enna O'Connor (10)   160
Lauren Handley (11)   161
Bonnie Airlie (11)   162
Dan Pease (11)   163
Emily Moss (10)   163
Tristan Mann (11)   164
William Lawson-Maycock (13)   165
Tasmine Graffy (10)   165
Abigail Lepine (12)   166
Rachel Bell (12)   167
Katharine Childs (12)   167
Lewis Crook (12)   168
Matthew Carmichael (12)   169
Sam Grantham (11)   169
Lucie Kibblewhite (12)   170
Lucy Seymour (12)   170
Victoria Etheridge (12)   171
Maxine Kwok (12)   172
Joe Russell (11)   173
Max Hardie (12)   173
Johanna Stevens-Yule (11)   174
Ellen Friend (12)   175
Jess Rolland (11)   176
Lee Baker (12)   176

The Angmering School

Jasmine Smith (11)	200
Naomi Horn (11)	200
Sam McCarthy (11)	200
Ryan Tester (11)	201
Robert Bishop (11)	201
Lucy Sambrook (13)	202
Charlotte Turner (11)	203

The Poems

Stomach Ache

One day I had a stomach ache,
So I asked my mother, 'Why?'
She said, 'It might be something that you ate.'
This was my reply,

'Well I had . . .
Cold alphabet spaghetti in the morning,
Green and mouldy bread at noon,
Ten-year-old boiled eggs for dinner
And I think I might've eaten the spoon!'

Peter James Humphreys (11)

Seasons

Winter comes when autumn goes,
Winter comes and pinches your toes,
It makes the garden bare and brown,
It makes you sad and makes your frown.

Spring comes with sprouting flowers,
Blooming trees that form elegant towers.
It makes the garden fresh and sweet
And still looking lovely and neat.

Summer comes with long, lovely days,
With light that leads our every way.
It makes the garden sunny and bright,
It's perfect weather for flying our kite.

Autumn comes with a gust of wind,
Clearing away all those who have sinned.
It fills the garden with colour and noise,
Making lots of work for the gardener boys.

Rhiannon Dunlop (11)
Farlington School

I Hate My Little Sister

I hate my little sister,
She always gets her way,
When we have an argument
I never get my say.

I hate my little sister,
She play with all my toys.
When I do my homework,
She makes a lot of noise.

I hate my little sister,
When I'm not at home.
She sneaks into my bedroom
And hides my mobile phone.

I hate my little sister,
She always tells on me.
She messes up my bedroom;
It's just not fair, you see.

I hate my little sister,
I shout at her - she cries;
She goes out and tells her friends,
A million, trillion lies.

I love my little sister,
Really, I'm sure I do.
She is a pain, but family,
If I'm honest, then it's true.

Alice Pollock (11)
Farlington School

Seasons

The soft, sweet daffodils,
Do sway in the gentle breeze,
While the fresh, green grass,
Does shoot up through its icy crush.

The scorching summer sun,
Beats down on the ground
And shrivels up the green grass,
To make it a dusty brown.

The hot summer sun is drifting away
And on the trees the leaves
Are turning golden brown,
Then they fall on the crusty ground.

The hard, cold winter is setting in,
It encases the ground
With an icy coating,
Now winter is here, no grass will appear.

Joanna Moyers (11)
Farlington School

War Time

Since the bomber came, the town has been shut up.
The only light that comes, is sad light,
Light that is weeping over silent souls,
Souls that have been silenced forever amongst the rubble.
There is nothing moving in that sea of rubble,
Only the wind comes and laps through the old cobble arches,
No laughter rings there now.
The mug of tea still on the coffee table has long gone cold.
The dawn chorus has flown away,
Taking all happiness with it,
So now, sadness *rules*.

Laura Beresford Pratt (11)
Farlington School

Winter

It creeps upon us like a ghost,
It spreads across from coast to coast.
As we shop and prepare ourselves,
By stacking high our cupboard shelves
With warm drinks and hot food,
We get into a Christmas mood,
But why are we jolly?
Decorating homes, gathering holly,
Whilst out in the freezing cold,
Animals are being brave, being bold.
They have no fun till spring they wait
Digging holes to hibernate.
They curl up tight and fall asleep
They don't look out, not even a peep
To see a land enveloped in white,
All through the day, all through the night.
With snowflakes dancing like crystal flames,
Then gently resting on windowpanes,
As the icy wind fiercely blows
A crunching frost blankets meadows.
No one told us, there was no warning
We're on our own now
Winter's dawning.

Lara Jones (11)
Farlington School

The Journey

Sitting on a tree in the sun,
My crispy skin all brown,
Suddenly I dropped,
A crazy dancing monster picked me up,
Whizzing and twirling me in its arms.

I thought any minute I would drop, shrivel up,
There was no turning back I kept on dancing,
I knew some day I would make the journey down,
Floating peacefully, but not like this.

Then I felt myself fall, I was drifting downwards, it was time,
The dancing devil discarded me for a new partner,
From a sunbed to twirl dance with.

Relieved the awful journey had ended,
Sad it was time to die,
I felt myself curl in and shrivel.

Catriona Dunlop (11)
Farlington School

Hallowe'en

I'm so excited, it's Hallowe'en,
Scaring people, making them scream!
Heavy black costumes with the hairy mask,
We do a trick if people ask!
Carved out pumpkins and flickering candles,
Knocking on doors, people opening the handles.
Delicious sweets
All in a bag
From a nice lady dressed up as a hag!
Spiders on strings, black cats with wings,
All the rest of the year would not see these things!

Emily Humphrey (11)
Farlington School

Hide-And-Seek

Bruises dotted across my back
Cuts dug deep into my brow,
Pains darting through my battered chest
I wish I were dead.

My heart still pounding,
My head still throbbing,
My legs still running,
He's still chasing.
I don't think he'll ever stop.

I run
He follows,
I hide
He seeks,
I stop
He stops,
I scream
But it's too late.

Alyssa Bacon (11)
Farlington School

Rainbow Poem

The rainbow is created by the rain and the sun
Like rushes of colour shot from a gun
You can see a rainbow from miles away
That's when little children come out to play
Red, yellow, purple, orange, green, blue and pink
Painted on the sky like strokes of ink
All those colourful rays in the sky
The rainbow shines from way up high
Eventually the rainbow will disappear
And the sky will be completely clear.

Emily Avery (11)
Farlington School

The Coldest Touch

Snowflakes dance down from the endless periwinkle sky,
Glistening orbs being chased by the whispering breeze,
Kissing my pale cheeks as they gracefully glide by,
Weaving around the numb arms of emotionless trees.
The familiar crunch of snow underfoot surrounds me,
A bitter chill settling over the distant countryside,
Church steeples veiled in crisp, white snow for all to see,
Winter's picturesque scene spreading far and wide.

Contented families glide dreamily across the glazed ice,
Tranquil laughter filling the bleak December air,
The carefree atmosphere making them so easy to entice,
Leaping daintily together without the smallest care.
As the keen winter is welcomed by the shimmering haze,
All become peaceful and will to offer so much,
Darkness arrives earlier absorbing the iciest of days,
Snow falls harmoniously and spreads the coldest touch.

Lottie Gammie (14)
Farlington School

Nature

Flowers and trees,
Bugs and bees,
Streams and rivers,
Clouds and givers.

Houses and traffic,
Towns and cities,
Streets and alleyways,
Cars and pollution.

Flowers and trees,
Bugs and bees,
Streams and rivers,
Clouds and givers.

That's what makes the world go round!

Stephanie McCabe (11)
Farlington School

Almost Cinderella

Holds her hand, stands by her side
Their smiles are so untrue,
All night long he whispers soft,
'Don't cry; it doesn't become you.'

They float across the floor,
As perfect as can seem,
But in her ear, he says, 'Remember:
Don't cry; it doesn't become you.'

The clock strikes twelve; the dance is done,
Cinderella's time is over,
Yet his words repeat in her mind -
'Don't cry; it doesn't become you.'

She wanders home in the darkness,
Snowflakes fall down around her,
But she holds her tears like frozen diamonds,
Because crying doesn't become her.

Camilla Brathwaite (17)
Farlington School

The Mirror

A sullen face,
Lost of expression,
No aim in life,
No ambition.

Rough complexion,
No sparkling eyes,
So sore, chapped lips,
Afraid to smile.

Now just the same,
The years were not kind,
With scars for life,
Through the memories.

Claire Mack (11)
Farlington School

If I Lost Tomorrow

(In loving memory of Grandpa)

If I lost tomorrow,
Would they know I'm gone?
Never, ever coming back
Could they still go on?

If I lost tomorrow,
Who's left for her to turn to?
No shoulder for her to lean on
How would she pull through?

If I lost tomorrow,
Would he really care?
Do you think he'd even notice
If I wasn't there?

'If you lost tomorrow,
We'd try to struggle through,
The lonely times ahead of us,
Our strength would come from you.

If you lost tomorrow,
There'd be no chance to see
Those many precious moments,
That meant so much to me.

We know there's no tomorrow
For soon you will be gone,
But in our hearts and minds and souls,
Your spirit will live on.'

Is there time to ask them,
Before I'm called away?
Will I be part of their tomorrows,
Or only their today?

Olivia Barclay-Hudson (11)
Farlington School

My Seasonal Sound Box

As I open my box I can hear . . .
The sparkling of the dew
As the leaves dance merrily past it.
I can hear the birds as they chatter
About the coming summer.
I enjoy listening to the wind,
As it soars across the sky,
Singing silently to itself;
And if I listen very closely,
I can hear the faint sound of the old oak,
As it whispers to the leaves
That are dancing around at its feet.

Suddenly, everything changes,
As the storm starts to approach.
Now I can hear the alarmed insects,
Scurrying in the jungle
Of overgrown grass,
As the daunting storm closes in.
The hailstones look like giant boulders,
Tearing up the sky as they soar
Noisily down to Earth;
And if I really listen,
I can hear the struggling sun
Determinedly fighting its way
From behind the destructive, deadly,
But at last, defeated clouds.

Lucinda Mitchell (11)
Farlington School

The Cruel Side Of Autumn

I was young then,
I didn't know the truth,
I had heard of something called autumn,
No one ever spoke of it,
No one would tell what it was,
But I soon found out,
It was not long before I began to wish
That autumn didn't exist.

The days were getting colder, windier and wetter,
Then I realised that the thing I had been dreading
All my life, was here,
It was now autumn.

Now it was my turn to go,
A strong gust of wind swept me away,
I tried to hold on, but I could not.

Lying on the cold earth underneath my tree,
I closed my eyes and took my last breath,
I was gone,
My life as a leaf was now over.

Matilda Sims (11)
Farlington School

Tom The Cat

Poor Tom the cat, his master told him to, 'Scat!
To go away and never come back.'
So Tom did take his advice
And sought out a career chasing mice
And from that day on, Tom had a ball
And he didn't miss his master at all!

Lottie Mungavin (11)
Farlington School

I Just Sit There In The Class

I just sit there in the class,
Waiting for the time to pass,
History, biology goes through my mind,
My class teacher seems very kind.

I just sit there in the class,
Waiting for the time to pass,
Spellings, science, my mind's buzzing,
So many subjects, my mind's fuzzing.

I just sit there in the class,
Waiting for the time to pass,
Literature, language, what do I do now?
Got to finish all my homework, somehow.

I just sit there in the class,
Waiting for the time to pass,
Suddenly, the bell rings, now I'm gone,
Each of these days is very long.

Emma Kulin (12)
Farlington School

Poor And Rich

The rich do not care about the poor in the town,
As they walk past they just frown.
Having no heart for people with less power,
They just look down from their tall, rich tower.

The poor just wonder about their moneyless future,
Steeling scraps of meat from the local butcher.
Begging for money at every corner,
Dreaming some day they will have their own sauna.

The fight continues between rich and poor,
With nobody willing to open the door,
The poor live in hope as the rich will get richer,
The two will remain with their personal feature.

Maria Doljikova (11)
Farlington School

Farlington Farm!

Throw your bags down at eight o'clock,
Pull you gloves on, don't you stop.
I've got the chickens out of bed,
Now to Willow, she has to be fed.

Scoop of oats into the bowl,
Watch her wolf them all down, whole.
Stay back Wilf, stay right back,
Just leave her to eat her little snack.

What about the chicken's food?
Oh no, Willow's in a mood.
She wants another bowl of oats,
Now that's not fair, you're just one goat!

I'm off now it's half-past eight,
Come on now, I can't be late.
You've had your food and your water,
I'm not your own personal porter!

Isabel Johnston (12)
Farlington School

Mist

Through the mist I stumble,
As I creep along the way.
I grab a leaf it crumbles.
I heard the call of the jay
This was ere the month of May.

The wind whips my face,
As it hurries along the road.
It seems to be on a chase
And put in first gear mode.
Would it not be wonderful
If everything just flowed?

Florence Beckett (12)
Farlington School

Working On Ice

Working at the ice rink,
Sat behind panels of glass,
Nine o'clock to seven,
Endless tickets and change to pass.

Is this a life?
No excitement, no fun.
Stuck behind a counter,
Forced to watch everyone.

Longing for the hour,
That the clock will strike.
A prophecy of peace, of quiet,
The time the skaters do not like.

When ice shall reign
And past my face the wind will fly.
As I rejoice happily,
In *ice* and sky.

I fly, I swoop
And do not pay.
To go forwards, backwards,
To race, to play.

Oh for that hour,
I cannot wait.
But now I must
Sit out my fate.

Is it worth it?
A fair exchange?
An hour of freedom,
For ten of giving change?

But my mind drifts as ever, onto the ice
And I reply *yes,* without thinking twice.

Bethany Jones (12)
Farlington School

The Farmyard

Once upon a time there lived a small and very normal cow,
One day when the cow (whose name was Daisy),
Found the master being lazy,
She set herself the task,
(Until the master woke up at last),
Of helping out in the big pigsty
And teaching newborn birds to fly,
But when the cat let up the cry - *miaow*
'Go, cow, go, go quickly now,
For farmer's woken up,
Get all the pigs out of the hay,
'Cause today is the dreadful day when one must get the chop,
For they are so big, juicy and fat,
Farmer's going to make sausages,
Pork, bacon, you know them all.'
'But I thought farmer had stopped all that.
He hasn't done it in ages.'
'He didn't cease so quickly now you must call,
Call all the pigs so that they can escape.
'The pigs are our friends.'
'Yes, so we must make them amends,' mewed the cat.
'Okay,' mused the cow, 'I understand now.'
And she called as loud as she could
And all the pigs came running so fast, right to where farmer stood.

Marie-Claire Steven (13)
Farlington School

Fashion

What's the fashion today then?
How shall I do my hair?
Up or down, blonde or brown,
Or shall I have it just bare?

What's the trend today then?
What, oh what shall I wear?
Sandals and socks, shorts and smocks,
Or maybe just jeans if I dare!

What's really cool today then?
Which hobbies does everyone do?
Running and riding, swimming and gliding,
Or line dancing, could this be true?

What's mega hot today then?
Which film must I go and see?
I can't keep up with this fashion so,
I guess I'll just start being me!

Hannah Brodrick (13)
Farlington School

The Horse And Rider

The horse's hooves sounded down the track,
The rider jangled the horse's tack,
The horse was galloping as fast as it could,
Charging through the unwanted wood,
The rider looked nervously behind,
She was looking for something that she could not find,
The rider pulled on the reins and looked around,
They both heard a rustling sound,
Once again the horse was off at speed
And then from her neck the rider's beads
Fell to the ground beneath
And scattered all over the heath.

For the beads are still lying there today,
But where the horse and rider are, I cannot say!

Natasha Dillnutt (13)
Farlington School

Our Journey To School

As we go past hills and trees on our journey to school,
I watch the birds flutter by and the clouds float overhead,
Forming shapes and patterns.
As the sun shines through the clouds and the trees,
I watch the cars whizz past our bus,
As we make our journey to school.
The older girls in the back of the bus, talk endlessly,
I sit in silence, observing the beautiful scenery,
On our journey to school.

When it snows, the hills look magical,
Covered in a thick, white blanket.
The snowflakes fall slowly to the ground,
On our journey to school.
As we pull up in the school drive,
I don't want to leave this wonderful piece of tranquillity,
But I know there will be another,
Tomorrow on our journey to school!

Rebecca Ayling (13)
Farlington School

Bluebells

Joyfully, people talk of their brilliant beauty.
Silently swaying in the breeze.
Swiftly they dance to the jingle, jangle tones.
Elegantly dancing in their bright blue ball gowns.
Frantically darting to one another to tell them a rumour.
A carpet of blue whispers, whispering in the breeze.

Georgina Brehaut (11)
Farlington School

Why, What And Where?

I look to the sky
For answers I know not why,
I'm looking for inspiration.

The answers seem to come from there,
But who produced them, why and where?
What helps me understand?

When I'm discouraged I look to the ground,
No answers there can ever be found,
When I'm in my deepest darkness.

When happy, I laugh and dance and sing
And do all kinds of things,
But what makes my happiness flow?

I look out to space,
I dance with grace.
In the sky there's nothing to be seen,
In the ground, there's demons in me.

But when I look for the truth
Where should I look?
My eyes or my heart?

Caroline Swarbrick (13)
Farlington School

Woods In Season

Winter:

>The air is clear and still,
>The leaves are frosty and white,
>The animals are all asleep,
>The woods are cold and bright.

Spring:

>The air is fresh and dawn is breaking,
>The leaves are green and shooting,
>The animals are awakening,
>The woods are bright and new.

Summer:

>The air is hot and stuffy,
>The leaves are dry and shiny,
>The animals are awake and alive,
>The woods are dappled and shady.

Autumn:

>The air is cool and breezy,
>The leaves are orangey-gold,
>The animals are all dozy,
>The woods are beautiful and cold.

Chloe Davies (13)
Farlington School

The Cyclist

His sodden black T-shirt is stuck fast against him,
His curly, black hair plastered over his face,
His long, flared, black trousers slam wetly against him,
As he pedals onwards not slowing his pace.

He swerves right to get round a huge lake-sized puddle,
He skids and he slides on the slippery street.
I watch and I wonder just where he is going,
He's shopping or does he have someone to meet?

I gaze through the window, not pulling the curtains,
But growling and cursing the miserable day.
The rain's trying to get through the glass so it splashes me,
Slashes me, soaks me and sends me away.

I hear the clock ticking, I hear the light clicking,
The rain on the pane rushes down in a river.
I snuggle into my chair, hugging my teddy bear,
Though the fire's gold, I'm so cold that I shiver.

I pick up my cocoa and lounge by the fire,
Which flickers and crackles and blazes alight.
The cocoa turns over and spills all upon me,
I scream at the heat and the terrible fright.

But outside the window, the cyclist is freezing,
A car has passed by him and sprayed him, he's wet,
But he pedals on more determined than ever,
He'll get there, at least he's not given up, yet.

Felicity Jones (13)
Farlington School

We Are The Youth

We are the youth. To adults we seem a mystery,
But we know our culture, our identity, our history.
In order to become part of civilised society,
We must lose our identity and individuality.

Capitalism, communism - call it what you will -
Either way we must learn to smile as we kill.
Explain to me why we should do our best,
For people who keep us silent - oppressed?

Why should we continue to play the game
For people who don't even know our names?
I don't want to be stuck in an office day after day,
No matter how good the conditions and pay.

They say the youth of today are mindless thugs,
Blame it on our culture, clothes, music, drugs.
While their petty squabbles over race and religion
Are shown to us every day through television.

If you stand up for something in which you believe,
They dish out the punishment that they should receive.
You can't silence us all and make out we're fools,
For following our beliefs but breaking the rules.

The fat cats and bureaucrats fail to understand,
That we are not in the palms of their hands.
We will try to continue; fighting the fight,
For what's true, just, honest and right.

The youth of today are the adults of tomorrow.
I must admit that it fills me with sorrow
To think that, when we get dull and old,
We'll forget our youth and the spirit that told
Us to ignore the adults - teachers, parents, politicians
And enjoy our lives, make our own decisions.

If you want to see the wonder and beauty of youth,
Look around you and there is constant proof,
In our culture, our music, our joy, our sorrow.
The youth of today are the adults of tomorrow.

Holly Chard (17)
Farlington School

Hello

Whispers drift through the shadows,
I gaze out through the windows,
Whispers are calling me,
I can hear them following me.

I hear them call my name,
I hear myself call my name,
I turn around,
Look all around.

Crying reaches my ears,
Revitalising all my fears,
It's getting closer to me,
Coming for me.

I'm trapped in a paradox,
Looking out at an autumnal equinox,
Voices all around me,
Someone come and find me.

Hello!

Hayley Davies (13)
Farlington School

Fred

There once was a donkey called Fred,
Who decided to go to bed,
But when he got home he found a bone
And all of a sudden he was dead.

But when it came to his funeral,
His mum made a noise so unusual,
She shouted and sung,
Till it was over and done,
Then threw herself out of the window.

Joseph Bawn (12)
Hazelwick School

Love Is Sweet When You . . .

Love is sweet
When you cuddle the bears
So can I join you?

Love is sweet
When you eat chocolate
So can I have some?

Love is sweet
When you score at football
So can I play?

Love is sweet
When you go to town
So can I come too?

Love is sweet
When you paint the wall
So can I work with you?

Love is sweet
When you kiss goodnight
So can I kiss you?

Amie Stovell (12)
Hazelwick School

Butterfly - Haiku

The butterfly sleeps,
So gentle and delicate,
Not a glimpse, nothing.

David Smith (12)
Hazelwick School

Survivor

I'm a survivor
I found a fiver
Stepped on the bus and beat up the driver
Took all his money
Thought it was funny
I'm a survivor
I've still got my fiver
I'm a survivor
I found a fiver
Stepped on the bus and the driver beat me up
He thought it was funny
He took all my money
I'm not a survivor
I ain't got my fiver.

Dipesh R Patel (12)
Hazelwick School

By The Countryside

When I went down to the countryside,
In an ancient, wooden caravan did I hide,
I felt safe, cosy and warm,
The way we should feel in our farms,
The day was sunny and fun,
Then at night I got such a fright,
But only a tree was in sight.

Aimee Humphries (12)
Hazelwick School

Haiku Of Big Ben

Arms tick everyday.
Tall and lanky legged creature.
London is its home.

Martin Geddes-Jones (Mutungi)
Hazelwick School

What Teachers Wear In Bed!

It's anybody's guess
What teachers wear in bed at night,
So we held a competition
To see if any of us were right.

We did a spot of research,
Although some of them wouldn't say,
But it's probably something funny,
As they look pretty strange by day.

Our teacher's quite old-fashioned,
He wears a Victorian nightshirt,
Our sports teacher wears her tracksuit
And sometimes her netball skirt.

That new teacher in the infants
Wears bedsocks with see-through pyjamas,
Our deputy head wears a T-shirt
He brought back from the Bahamas.

Teachers wear funny clothing,
Think they are smart enough,
Teachers are nice, funny and fidgety,
But I like my school.

Shabana Khan (12)
Hazelwick School

Monster

He was big,
He was fat,
He was cuddly, like a bear.
He was hairy,
He was smooth,
He was a big monster from the moon.
He played with us,
He danced with us,
He ate and got fatter every day.
He was a monster,
He was a friend,
But we lost him at the end.

Asim Zafir (12)
Hazelwick School

Cat

Lies low, prowling
In the dark, silent, night
Only seen by street light
Hunting, killing, innocent prey.

Lies on your lap
Happy, so he purrs
Sits still and never stirs
Lazy and content is this cat.

Slick, silky fur
Green eyes, shine bright
Always getting into fights
Independent is this cat.

He hunts, he fights
Stays inside all day
Sometimes he might want to play
There, forever, is this cat.

Rhiannon Hart (13)
Ifield Community College

Fishing

I went to a fishing shop
And bought some bait.
I then went to a fishing lake,
Called New Pound.

I got all of my gear
Out of my mum's car
And started to walk to my swim,
I had a good look at the lake
To see who was where
Has anyone caught a fish?

I got to my swim,
The first thing I do is
To see if there are any snags in my swim
Then I look out for any signs of a pike.

I then set up my rod
I was using one rod for carp
And I used my 9m pole for
Tench and bream.

The bait I was using
On the pole,
Was small, juicy pellets
And red maggots.

And on my carp rod
I had scopex bollies
And mixed pellets.

At the end
Of my fishing day
I had five carp
All around about 5lbs
And a few tench and bream.

Gareth Daniels (15)
Ifield Community College

What Is A . . . ?

What is a friend?
What is a mate?
Sometimes they are early
They even might be late
But you can wait because they're your mate.
What is a friend?
What is a mate?
Sometimes you are the best of buddies
Sometimes things are worse
But it'll work out if your relationship has no curse.
What is a friend?
What is a mate?
They lend you their best CD
And then you lend them yours
But that's known as part of the friendship course.
What is a friend?
What is a mate?
They call you on the phone
And text you too because they know you have no money
But they want to keep in contact with you.
What is a friend?
What is a mate?
You say hello each morning
You say goodbye each night
Look at your relationship with your friend it might be a terrible fright.

Dean Hayward (16)
Ifield Community College

Grandad's Funeral

Two weeks ago my grandad died
He had serious heart problems
But there was nothing the hospital could do.
Four days later
The funeral was held
In a church in the country.
The day was beautiful
Like a flower blooming in spring,
Birds were singing
The wind was brushing the branches
Of the trees.
The service was sad because everyone was crying
And upset and people had to do speeches.
Afterwards we went outside where my
Grandad would be buried.
We all stood around the prepared grave
My grandad's gateway to a certain place
No one knew where.
After the coffin was lowered and at rest
We all put an object into the hole
Just something we associated with him.
I put a watch in there that I had bought for
His eightieth birthday.
Then we walked away, heads down.
I wish he was still alive
He was not supposed to die.

Daniel Petch
Ifield Community College

Outside

I sit looking through my window at the outside
Trees swaying, grass shifting
The land is continuous over miles wide
While birds sit in treetops and just sing, sing, sing.

I want to go out, run and play
Play with my friends in the wide, green fields
Just play and play with no cares all day
When I return home I will feel all relaxed and chilled.

I watch the cows pick at the grass
Sheep rolling, playing with each other
Horses running together to see which one is fast
Pigs grunting in dire attention from their mother.

As the sun is about to set
I see a distant shadow of birds flying away
Now my day is up I am off to bed
Dreaming of this marvellous day.

Nathan Pawlak (14)
Ifield Community College

The Drunken Man

The drunken man
Stumbled down the dramatic street
The street candles tidy his eyes
As a terrified shoulder disturbs him
The drunken man struck
The white murder was a sea
Of blood-curdled petals.

The drunken man collapsed
In shock, but smiled
The dead stranger stares him in the face.
Anger takes over his conscience,
The Grim Reaper arrived in his imagination
With an eager look on his face.

Lauren Hall (14)
Ifield Community College

Stream Of Consciousness, London's Night

White, snowy rock, sizzling in the underground,
Gushing history of the
Hard cliff petals.

Rock-winding Thames,
Beams blue salt, up, down
The square of words.

Big Ben, sprouting sunflower,
Below, bees freezing pebbles
Hot, sweaty fish, jumping miles
For blane to cliff,
The wind.

Trafalgar's waters carry
The life of royalty such
As enormous stems pierce
The lonely paws of the lions.

Hayley Woollard (13)
Ifield Community College

The Football Fight

As I stepped out to see this sight
The sun was shining very bright.
The crowd roared
As I got floored
Then I started a fight.

As I calmed down
His face was all brown
Covered in lots of mud.
I felt the blood
And then fell down with a thud.

I found myself in bed
With cuts all over my head.
I turned to my nurse
She said it could have been worse!

Liam Campbell (14)
Ifield Community College

Friends Are Forever

Friends are forever don't let them down,
Because one day they won't be around,
Keep them locked in your heart,
So then you won't drift apart,
They're special in every way,
So tell your friends how much you really care,
About them everyday:

To my friend, I say this now,
I can't pretend to show you how,
How much you really mean to me,
I love you more than each wave on the sea,
I love you more than each leaf on a tree,
Just knowing you loved me would set my heart free,
Because my love for you will never die,
I'll save a place for you in the sky,
So when you move on you will remember me,
I'm the one, who took the time,
To send the angels from up high,
To come down and make this rhyme,
So when you read it your heart will fly,
As close to me as it can,
So you know I'm your biggest fan.

So tell your friends how much you care,
Because true friends are really rare!

Lauren Harms (14)
Ifield Community College

Communication

A teenager's way of life,
Buttons being sucked in, popping out,
Travelling, travelling . . . sent!
Beep, beep! One new message,
Eyes focused, phone vibrates,
Reply.

Pointing at the box,
Light flashes, static flicker of the screen,
Appears my programme.
Curl up in my chair, relax . . .
And watch.

Purchase the gossip,
Flick through the pages,
Dissolve in the stories, gasp at the problems,
Giggle at the embarrassing moments,
Finished within an hour.

Modem kicks in, dialling . . .
Connected! *Click, click* as the arrow
Darts across the screen, flowing with
Your hand, mirroring your command.
Search found!

Faye Rabson (14)
Ifield Community College

Friends

Friends are here
Friends are there
Talking and gossiping
Like they don't care.

Friends who cry
Friends who laugh
Running and walking
Down the path.

Friends with pride
Friends who hide
Shouting and snogging
Round the side.

Friends who come
Friends who leave
Driving and travelling
To see me?

Friends are true
Friends who lie
Wise and old
Those who try.

Friends who stand by ya
Friends who die
Love and trouble
You just wanna sigh.

Friends who work
Friends who give up
Time and effort
They just want a pup.

Friends who you love
Friends who you hate
Honest or disloyal
But do you want a date?

Friends you need
Friends you don't
So don't forget
You're on your own!

Shelley Bowen (14)
Ifield Community College

The Cliffs For Dad

I stood on a cliff
With the clouds behind me
Then, in front, a blue ocean
As far as the eye can see.

As the sun set gleaming
My tears kept streaming
Waiting for my dad to return
Am I dreaming?

Looking at the horizon
As it went gold
Day became night
And my dream got old.

I started home, but when I got to the door
I saw a boat coming in far off shore
My feet rush me to the coast
Hoping I could identify it as it got close.

The sun had set, my tears stopped streaming
Instead I changed and started grinning
It's been three weeks since I saw him last
Now I can have fun among him and his cast.

Peter Biddle (15)
Ifield Community College

Childhood Fear!

Legend's colour, dreams and ghost,
His whisper, pain of childhood fear,
Pale fingers fall to terror blue,
The evil of childhood fear, blackens,
Flowers die as the shadow of light.
Whole light is uniform eyes of bright yellow.

Invisible pain and laughs, bring childhood fear,
Out of wind, work, it blackens
The shadows spore light, brings green earth,
Like a bat out of Hell, the tear holes in childhood fear.
I start at the top and fall, bring back the life
Everything starts at fear and grows, wild flies couldn't stop.

Childhood fear stays in shadows, like wind and fire.
Dragon's heart and fairy tales, blow wind, blow
Childhood fear whispers in his pain.
Bold letters, green skies, life and death
Childhood fear
Whispers down the way, in the screams of eight.

They, the shadows, whisper pain and laughter
They fear what they fear
Munch, munch they go, up the spine-tingling fear
Stop, stop they groan, louder and louder
Sense the soft, wrinkled fingers, appear the face of
Childhood fear.

The break of the skin, the darkness of evil, childhood fear
Underworld deep, the sun cracks in, like fairy-dust fear
People stop stress, relax, mind boggles on what's ahead
Childhood fear they bring
Happiness and joy, blood rivers float the boat of fear
Love, war, hate, fear, they bring *childhood fear!*

Katy Hickey (13)
Ifield Community College

Anonymous

Multicoloured rain fills the clouds in the sky.
A quick flash by the eye as death's light kills the wings.
Fall of night came as the runway to Hell opened its gates to the
circle of life.
Black clouds surrounded the morning light, the fierce, fiery doors
shut!
Leaves fell from the blossomed trees as the shadow creeps over
the grass.
Crashing lightning hit the clouds as the barking hurricane twirled
their way.
The rain fell as the lightning struck, the chipped water ragged
down the street, like a giant's footsteps . . .
The sky turned grey, as if night.
Who was this man?
We didn't know.
But he was destined to never be shown . . .

Lyndsey Fowlie (13)
Ifield Community College

The Hoop Is Eternal

Strong jump jagged, screams beautifully wild,
Great emotions stirring, striking as a teardrop,
Descends to earth - the teardrop is powerful
This day. In all means the conflict was the cause.

Joy: To hold the world In your grasp - down, up, up, down,
In and out aesthetic art rages war upon the auditorium. The
Black and white icons of the capsule environment, and yet
United and rejoicing through even sorrow which is
The basis of everything this arena is not.

Determination in us all; potent and focused, I embrace even
Those who strike me down.
Immune to pain - I have transcended the boundaries of
Physical and mental achievement.

Markos Patrick Rossiter (16)
Ifield Community College

Daydream

In a story I was writing at school,
My writing didn't seem to make sense at all!
I sat and imagined what life would be,
To be a dolphin deep in the sea
I had a blue body and I had a small head
I found that some rocks would soon be my bed!
I saw all of my friends, they were creatures too!
Michelle was a green fish and Rosy was blue.

I swam a bit far and couldn't go back
I didn't have a watch, so of the time, I lost track.
Then I discovered what life really was,
Cold and dark, life the mystery of oz.
Then a small crab came up to me,
'Excuse me young lady, would you join us for tea?'
Normally I hate crabs, but I thought *why not?*
And followed the crab who was doing a trot.

The crab lived in a cave, such a magical place,
The young crab himself stared at my face.
'Excuse me young lady, don't mean to be rude,
But your long mouth seems to have come, er, unglued!'
I looked in a mirror and then I could see,
That surely, but slowly, I was turning back into me!
'Thanks Mr Crab,' I said as I handed him cash,
The dinner was lovely, but I really must dash!

And with that, I swam far away,
I was so worn out, I'd had such a long day
As I went to the surface, my oxygen was running out
I could no longer breathe, so I gave a big shout!
I came back from my daydream and began to write my invention,
But Mr Howarth came over and said, 'Right. Detention!'

Sarah Manners (13)
Ifield Community College

She Was Gone

She chose to walk alone.
Though others wondered why.
She refused to look before her.
Her eyes cast toward the sky.
The birds flew and whispered.
That she only wanted freedom.
From what she felt were puppet strings.

She opened her arms long and wide.
While the sunlight brightly shone through.
The sky refused to tell.
How she would hide so well.
But everyone woke up one day.
To find that she was gone.

She chose to walk alone.
Though others wondered why.
She refused to look toward her.
Her eyes cast towards the sky.
The birds flew and whispered.
That she only wanted freedom.
From what she felt were puppet strings.

Longing to be free.
She watched the birds fly gracefully.
Always urging to soar in the clouds.
She would wish up on the glittery stars.
For the wish to be free from her puppet strings.
Could it only remain as a dream?

Some say she wished too hard.
Some say she wished too long.
But everyone woke up one day
To find that she was gone.

Kerrie Bailey (14)
Ifield Community College

Tomorrow Comes After The Dark

With untruths untold you intrude my life,
Afflicting your lies like a tormented soul.
To bruise me, to wound me,
Is that what you brought here for.
I never knew betrayal, but it came disguised as you.
Like a disease you ate at my heart.
And you questioned my hostility?
I despised you with a passion.
Misery filled my body and flowed through limb to limb till
I was numb.
It was like a depression.
To grieve, to be sad and sorrowful,
It was not I, but what I had become.
Change. Morph. Transform.
However you wish to interpret it I rejected your supposed
Love.
I became strong.
And it was because of my faith, my trust, my belief that
Tomorrow will only come after the dark.

Sophie Dowdeswell (16)
Ifield Community College

Poem

The children come home, the door flies open, the hum
Of the children flies through the home.
Grazing of knees,
A hair-pull and a slap,
A hitch up satchel,
A pulled down cap,
As the sound goes flat.

Lawrence Clarke (12)
Ifield Community College

No Time To Tell You

When I look up at the starry night sky
My heart fills with a sudden rush of love
I may never be able to say goodbye
But I will see you from way up above.

I can't describe how much you mean to me
I love you with my heart and always will
You never knew you were too blind to see
My heart feels like it is lying still.

I wanted to know if you felt the same
But before I knew it, it was too late
It was so sudden, no one was to blame
The doors opened for you at Heaven's gate.

I wish I'd told you how much I loved you
Then maybe you'd have felt the same for me too.

Rachel Stamps (16)
Ifield Community College

Emotions, Why?

Emotions,
Sometimes they hurt,
They can cause a lot of pain,
But that feeling of love, it can't be resisted
Or the feeling of anger just seeing red,
When you've no control left,
Emotions,
Sometimes they can be so mixed and confused,
The temptation just to let go,
Jealously, anger, love, hate, passion, envy . . .
Why do we feel these things?
Is it because we have heart, mind, body and soul
Or just because . . .
We were made to feel?

Emma-Louise Barling (15)
Ifield Community College

Poems

Writing a poem is not as easy as it looks
Even though I've read loads of books.
Must do this homework before I can have fun
Oh will my work ever be done?

Sitting wondering about what to write
Agonising day and night
Ideas have not yet come
Oh will my work ever be done?

I've got a poem but it won't rhyme
Now I'm rapidly running out of time
'Dinner's ready,' shouts my mum
Oh will my work ever be done?

I've been here hours, it's getting late
But good things come to those who wait
Dark disappears and up comes the sun
Oh will my work ever be done?

Finally a piece of inspiration
Write it all down as confirmation
My poem's done and it's nearly Sunday
Now I'm ready, bring on Monday.

Sarah Grubb (15)
Ifield Community College

Dragons

D ragonheart a famous dragon,
R iding high in the sky,
A nd tearing flames through his nostrils,
G uiding St Lancelot to the villages,
O ver the hills Dragonheart flies,
N othing stops Dragonheart falling about,
S t Lancelot and Dragonheart are falling on villages.

Chantal Roberts (13)
Ifield Community College

Bullied

From the smile on her face,
You would never have known,
That even in the biggest crowd,
She could feel so alone.

Even as her smiles fades
And down her face the tears cascade,
No one sees or even cares,
About the pain she hides and never shares.

She has been stabbed in the back,
People only want the things she lacks,
No one cares that she is crying
And no one knows inside she's dying.

But she still holds on tight,
Comes through darkness into light,
She smiles as the pain drifts away,
The fight is over for another day.

Holly Marshall (15)
Ifield Community College

A Dragon

A dragon is the wind in your hair,
A dragon is an arrow in the air,
A dragon is a mosaic of patterns,
A dragon is a Chinese lantern.

A dragon wants to live loud,
A dragon wants to live proud,
A dragon wants to stay alive,
But failed in its attempt to survive.

Robert Cooper (12)
Ifield Community College

I Promise

I've never found a love so deep,
A love as strong as ours,
This promise unto you I keep,
I'll forever be your baby.

The promise that I make to you,
A symbol of my love,
Is showing you my love is true
And proving I'm your baby.

I searched for love and now you're found,
I'm never letting go.
A promise means our hearts are bound,
I'll always be your baby.

The promise you placed upon my hand,
Around my wedding finger,
Is a promise that will forever stand,
To show I am your baby.

And if the promise ever breaks
And tears my soul to pieces;
Ignore the cries my heart makes,
It's lost its only baby.

So if we're ever torn apart,
Over any reason,
Find a place within your heart
And always remember your baby.

Amy Tucker (16)
Ifield Community College

Autumn

The cool breeze whistles through me,
Making me reach for my gloves,
The chilly air washes across my face,
My breath comes out in frosted ice.

A tree captures my attention,
It is swaying in the wind,
I watch as a leaf gently falls,
Finally gracing the pavement.

It falls near my feet,
I study the fine details on it,
Rich reds, oranges and golds,
Merge together, making it shine.

The strong wind carries the leaf away,
I watch as it disappears into the night,
Where will it go next?
Who will find it?

Now the night is starting to darken,
I should get home, cosy fire and warm food awaits me,
As I think of these things, I feel so lucky,
Luckier than the leaf.

Victoria Findlay (15)
Ifield Community College

The Storm

Wind howling, windows rattling,
I carry on walking, constantly battling,
Through the wind and rain,
Here comes the hailstones, ouch! The pain.

Lightning cuts through the sky like a knife
And robs a tree of its life,
A clap of thunder fills the air
And the sky turns as black as a witch's hair.

'Never put up your umbrella' my nan used to say,
As you could get blown across the bay,
I don't want to fly as high as a kite,
Even though Mary Poppins might!

As I turn into my street,
The puddles splash over my feet,
Rubbish blows all over the place,
An empty crisp bag hits me in the face.

As I walk up my garden path,
A stray branch catches hold of my scarf,
It gets blown up into the sky
And the storm eats it up like a piece of pie.

I step into my house, it's lovely and warm,
I'm glad to escape that terrible storm,
I'm a lot luckier than Dorothy was,
She ended up in the land of Oz!

Melissa Wright (16)
Ifield Community College

The Storm

The storming howling, crashing
It came from over seas.
The storm howling, thundering
Over land and through trees.

The storm howling, thundering
Torrential rain pounding the ground.
The storm howling, crashing
Every little space was found.

The storm howling, crashing
The lightning became frightening.
The storm howling, thundering
Down came the hailstones lightly.

The storm howling, thundering
Every house and building down.
The storm howling, crashing
Flooding every little space found.

The storm howling, thundering
Making way towards land.
The storm howling, crashing
Leaving a trail of sound and sand.

The storm howling, crashing
Uprooting trees and leaves.
The storm howling thundering
Even killing bees.

Until everything went still and silent
And the storm went crashing out.

Elaine Willoughby (15)
Ifield Community College

I Will Always Love You!

(Dedicated to Michael Roberts)

To be in love, what does that mean
Or do you just say it to keep me keen?
When you say it, does it come from the heart?
Which mine will break if we were to part.

Because I believe that you are the one
When we're together, we have so much fun,
When you're near, my day seems lightened
With you around, I never feel frightened.

We've had some arguments, but they don't matter
Our love will stay strong and never shatter,
We'll be together for eternity
In love forever, we will be.

I remember the day when we first met
I wanted you and my mind was set,
You were perfect, but could you see
Just how much you'd mean to me?

Then the day came when we started to date,
You were more than my boyfriend, you were my best mate,
We're still together to this very day
And still, we will be when we're old and grey.

I will do all that I can
To ensure that you will stay my man,
We'll stay together, just us two,
Remember darling, that I will always love you!

Rebecca Jones (15)
Ifield Community College

Girl Guiding

Rainbows at 5,
Brownies at 7,
Guides at 10,
Senior section at 14,
Adult leaders at 18
And the GGA goes on and on.
In the GGA everyone has fun,
No one ever pulls out,
There are many interesting badges,
As well as many camps.
Everyone takes part and
Has many fun adventures,
The promise has three parts,
To say it you must know the sign.
The promise badge has the same design,
It varies in colour from sector to sector.
Every meeting there is a Brownie ring,
As well as Brownie bells to say goodnight.
Every unit has a Guider,
An assistant Guider,
A unit helper,
A young leader
And a pack leader,
They all help to run a unit.
Rainbows end at 7,
Brownies end at 10,
Guides end at 14,
Senior Section ends at 18
Adult Leaders ends at 65.

Lena Robinson (15)
Ifield Community College

Please Leave My Mind

Voices chatting in my head
An incessant barrage of sound
Voices of angels, voices of the dead
Never in here will peace be found.

Bright swirling patterns constantly turn
Spinning every which way
A hole in my brain will these images burn
If they don't vanish some day.

A devil with a pitchfork, deep inside
The canals of my grey, twisted brain
Stabbing me as he walks with every stride
His desire, to have me slain.

All these noises, pictures and intruders
Heed this message you find
Go now, for I will be deluded
Please leave my mind.

Alice Crane (15)
Ifield Community College

The Salmon

Swimming against the current up the waterfall,
You see the salmon giving it its all,
Trying, trying, getting nowhere,
Hurry up salmon here comes the bear!
The bear runs off, he tries again, he makes it up,
But as soon as he's up,
He dies, back down again,
Dead, dead, easy food for the bear,
Once he eats, blood smothers the air.

'Have a break, have a Kit-Kat'.

Jamie Nelson (14)
Ifield Community College

My Cat

My cat's ginger, full of hair,
I always pass him on the stair.

Fur like a teddy,
Teeth like nails,
He runs round the garden like a train on rails.

Catching birds,
Catching mice,
My cat isn't very nice.

Stripes like a tiger,
Voice like a mouse,
He's always running around the house.

He follows me here,
He follows me there,
He follows me everywhere.

He's always sitting on the wall,
Standing there very tall,
He looks up and down,
Round and round,
Oh no, what has he found?

So that's the story of my cat,
Now sitting here on the mat.

Amy Killick (12)
Ifield Community College

A Day At The Match

The football match starts
The whistle has blown,
It may not be long
Till a red card is shown.

How many goals
Will your team score today?
Are they playing at home
Or have you travelled away?

The home crowd go mad
As their team try to score,
The goalkeeper saves it
And falls to the floor.

There goes the whistle
It signals off-side,
It wouldn't have mattered
The shot was well wide.

When you see supporters
Up in the crowd
It makes you want to
Join in and sing loud.

The fans go wild,
A goal, hooray!
Perhaps their team
Will win today.

It won't be long,
Till the whistle goes,
The managers are nervous
It really shows!

At last the game has come to an end,
Roll on next week, will you attend?

Amy Cole (13)
Ifield Community College

Full Moon

Full moon, full moon,
Shining bright,
What a beautiful sight,
In the middle of the night.

Full moon, full moon,
Floating in the starry sky,
Illuminating all as you go by.

Full moon, full moon,
So great and bold,
More precious than gold,
Is your other side dark and cold?

Full moon, full moon,
That is it for now,
See you next time you come around.

Louisa Zuccarello (12)
Ifield Community College

The End Of School

When the bell rings at 3 o'clock
The children come out in a flock,
I fill with glee,
My brother is merrily,
Because it is the end of the day,
Now we can go out to play,
But when I stay in, I don't have a grin
And I get bored right up to my chin,
Then I do my homework so I can hand it in,
That way I get more merits so I can win.

Daniel Austin (12)
Ifield Community College

The Solar System

Earth is like a patchwork quilt,
It's in the shape of a circle,
It goes round and round,
Like a patchwork quilt.

Venus is like a round orange,
It's like a bouncy hot ball,
It's like a small, round fireball,
It goes round and around.

Sun is like a fireball,
Shining in the sky.

Mercury is like a silver moon,
Lighting up the sky.

Pluto is like a silver ball bearing
Glistening in your eye.

Saturn is like a yellow flower,
With lots of circles around it
The glistening of the flower,
With buzzing bees humming around it.

Mars is like the chocolate button,
Yummy enough to eat,
Brown chocolate button,
Glistening in your eye.

Jupiter is like a disco ball,
Glistening in your eyes,
Like a silver gel pen,
Glistening at night.

Uranus is like a dull sky,
Very dull sky.

Neptune is like a purple ball,
Bouncing, bouncing,
Far away, out of reach.

Zoë Smith (12)
Ifield Community College

My First Day At ICC

My first day at ICC,
I thought it was well scary!

I couldn't wait to try on my blazer,
I couldn't wait to try on my tie,
I couldn't wait to get my planner,
I knew that I'd be flying high!

I was scared of the teachers,
I was scared to make friends,
I was scared of how I looked,
But I had the best luck in the end!

I was unsure of the building,
I was unsure of the names,
I was unsure of the lockers
And where we'd have games!

I got lost in the lessons,
I got lost in our lines,
I got lost with my mates,
But now I know my way fine!

People like me,
People think I'm funny,
People like the way I look,
I really love ICC.

Gaynor Marie Fitzsimons (12)
Ifield Community College

Dragon Knight

The dragon blew a flame out of his nostril
And the knight threw his sword side to side,
The dragon climbed a mountain,
With a mouth like a fountain,
Which gave the knight plenty of time to try and hide.

Wayne Heath (12)
Ifield Community College

A Lost Friend

At the beginning there were three
One on one, on one
There were three.
Through good and bad
There were three.
One day
One said to Two,
'Three does not like you.'
So One and Two were through with Three
Three was gone
Now there were two
Side by side
Through good and bad
There were two
One got bored with Two
So the famous three were not three
Who should we blame
One, Two or Three?

Moral of the story,
Pick your friends
One by one by one.

John Brady (15)
Ifield Community College

My First Loss

I had a dog for about ten years but then one day it got lost
I did not see or find him for two months then I went for
A walk on a winter's day.
It was cold and cloudy. Then I saw him.
I was positive it was my dog. I called him by his name.
He came bounding towards me,
I felt on top of the world,
It brought tears to my eyes,
It was the happiest day of my life.

Ben Seymour (14)
Ifield Community College

Henry's First Three Loves

His dead brother's wife,
Got married to Arthur's successor,
But Henry was not grateful,
About the child that was to succeed him.

Henry fell in love,
With a dark-haired beauty,
Anne Boleyn was to be Catherine's replacement,
However, the church refused divorce.

Henry took sudden action
And took over the Catholic Church,
Anne Boleyn was Catherine's replacement,
But the marriage ended in treason.

Henry had a second daughter,
Elizabeth by name,
He fell in love with his deceased wife's mistress,
Jane Seymour was his flame.

At last an heir was born,
But the happiness was not to last,
His beloved flame burnt out
As Jane Seymour lay there, dead.

Dee-Dee Edlin (15)
Ifield Community College

Dragons

D ragons are fire-breathing reptiles,
R oaring as loud as a whistle,
A ggravating villagers when it destroys homes,
G oing around eating people like a shark having its raw meat,
O ver the village it will fly like an eagle waiting for its prey,
N asty villagers try to destroy this amazing creature,
S ee this creature as it flies above your head like a giant mountain.

Craig Hampson (12)
Ifield Community College

Why Am I Here?

She felt all flustered,
Just from thinking,
Everything in my life has gone wrong,
Seeing him was a blunder,
Which is now a dilemma,
I've got to hold my head up high and be strong.

I used to cry at night,
Or when I saw his face,
He gave me a feeling,
That I didn't need to feel,
I thought, *what was my meaning?*
Why was I here?

I looked at his picture,
He made me smile,
But not for long,
I thought, *what might he say?*
If I saw him again,
Maybe one day soon
Or even today.

Sharon Reddin (15)
Ifield Community College

You Got Money!

We all went to the same school,
We ate the same food,
What did you do to get all that money?
Now you look at me as if you never knew me,
I was once your friend but not any more.

I am wise, I read hard and I got a better job,
Please give me some money!
All the cars you have got
You've got everything you want,
Why not give us some?

Chris Kizza (14)
Ifield Community College

Do You Know The Answer?

A man is a man
Whatever his colour
Race
Culture
People are different
All over the world
We are all Earth's children
Why shouldn't we share it?
As flowers differ
We human beings differ
We are taught the same
We eat the same
Why has difference become a barrier?
A barrier that prevents sanity
A barrier that locks if in ignorance
Why should our appearance matter?
Why should anything matter to us?
Are human beings doomed to be
Power hungry?
Do we need power to live?
No indeed we don't
Then why are we so?
Is the answer ever given?
Without an answer,
We give way to conflicts,
The more we give way
The small conflicts turn into huge wars
I am not saying we should agree on everything
But why give way to such insanity
Do you know the answer?
I certainly don't know!

Shangeethaa Sangaralingham (15)
Ifield Community College

The Man Of A Thousand Blades

This man
He sits in the dark
Waiting for the time
The time when he passes on
On to what lies beyond this consciousness
He waits and waits but it does not come
But still he sits and waits
Waiting for the inevitable to come.

His life
He has led a life
Like every other person
However, this life is different from the rest
This life is filled with anger, misery and sorrow
These are the only things this man knows
Nothing else is relevant
That is why he waits
His life is pointless so he sits and waits.

He gives up waiting
He gets up off his waiting chair
He saunters into the kitchen
He looks around for something sharp
Something sharp enough to end his torment
And take him as quickly as he was given.

All he sees is a room full of knives
Nothing more and nothing less than knives
But which one so many to choose from
He gathers them up and sorts them out
By size, by shape, by length, by width,
But still he has no clue, which one
Which one shall strike the fatal blow.

And where should it be
In the heart
In the stomach
Slit his wrists
So many places to choose from
So, which one will it be?
He tires of this rapidly
He loses interest and contemplates another plan
He trots back to his chair
He sits and waits
He waits but for another reason
He is thinking
Thinking how it could be done.
Swiftly into the heart
Or slowly, painfully across the wrist
Thinking, thinking, forever thinking.

Suddenly it comes to him
In his sorrow in his pain that is his life
So many different knives
So many different ways
Why not
All at once
As many knives in as many places
As many as his body will take.

He toggles into the kitchen
Assembles every knife he has
He sets them up
He ties them to some string and hoists them to the ceiling
All it would take is the snip of the scissors
One by one they are hoisted
Dangling from the ceiling
As tightly packed as possible.

He lay beneath them with the scissors of fate
He braces himself
He says a prayer and chops
The knives come crashing down in an instant
Each one different
Some sharp
Some blunt
Some rusted to the core
But all as deadly as the next.

In a second his life is gone
As quickly as it was given
He is gone
No more chair, no more sitting
All that is left is an empty shell
The shell of a broken man
The shell of a man who exists no more.

Ryan Beck (14)
Ifield Community College

Why?

Why is it that I linger in the desolation of your love?
The paradise I dream of will never come to be,
Why do I hold so tightly,
To that which draws away?
Why do I ignore the truth?
Why do I refuse to see? Romeo is long past dead,
His place is vast and empty,
Nothing left to feel but pain.
Joy is but a passing fancy,
Yet, forever, I persist,
Not an angel, nor a saint,
Simply a dreamer that never learnt to succumb.

Jessica McGregor (15)
Ifield Community College

Lighthouse!

The thousand stairs
And the blaring light
Which shines through every night
Loneliness, darkness, but also brightness,
Bright light
Lighthouse red and white.

Stairs to climb
Out of breath
Oh no
No rest
Switches, buttons,
Colourful lights,
But also sometimes gives us a fright.

Ships come in
And follow the light
Maybe a bit bright
They come through whatever the weather
Mist, rain, hailstones and snow too.

Francesca Miles (14)
Ifield Community College

The Angry Dragon

My dragon is angry, he sits alone in his den,
In a nasty contest, he gets 10 out of 10.

He glides around spitting balls of fire,
He's a great thief, but a terrible liar.

The villagers need help, so they call for a knight,
The dragon and him fought long through the night.

In the end the dragon is slain,
The slayer is gone, after getting paid.

Dominic Pollard (12)
Ifield Community College

They'll See

(Inspired by 'Education for Leisure' by Carol Ann Duffy)

I hate life
People always say
Don't do this
Don't do that
Sit up straight
What did I tell you?
One day I'll be telling them
One day they'll see
One day
Today
Today
I know I can show them
Today
They'll see
Today
Red hot anger
Today
White hot pain
Today
That's what they'll suffer
Today
Suffer
Today
They'll see.

Michelle Barnett (14)
Ifield Community College

Rolly

He's big, black and cuddly,
But very fidgety,
He's huge, strong and tough,
But is not that rough,
He looks like a bear,
Acts like a hare
And runs everywhere.

He bounces like a spring
And he ate my brand new ring,
My goods are all chewed up
Because he's only a pup.

He thinks he's one of us
Cos he sits on chairs
And makes a fuss.

My pup Rolly
Is lovely,
I shout and scream at him,
But he never gives up,
I love my pup to pieces
And I will never give him up!

Amy Hummerston (12)
Ifield Community College

Dragon

D angerous, deadly dragons,
R un fiercely through fields of green,
A ngrily they catch their prey,
G rabbing and tearing they eat,
O n they go, attacking things in their way,
N ight comes, they rest their heads and silence occurs.

Donna Light (12)
Ifield Community College

Lonely Stranger

It's a dark and starry night,
All the stars pointy and bright,
The white moon big and round,
Everything moves without a sound.

The river shining, a golden gleam,
The light shining down the stream,
The trees shadows, big and dark,
The swings shimmering in the park.

Suddenly footsteps begin to appear,
This man's dark face full of fear
He walks around on his own,
Muttering to himself in a gloomy tone.

His hair greasy and long,
His eyes wide and red,
Where was he going? This lonely man
With sweat dripping from his head.

He kept on walking
It seemed like hours,
His big long legs
Were like tall towers.

He began to run
Through the trees
Dodging the roots
Treading on dead leaves.

He disappeared into the night,
The stars all disappearing,
The moon had gone
And the sun was reappearing.

Jo Chubb (12)
Ifield Community College

Dragons

I love dragons
As big as wagons
They are nice and green
The best I've seen
When they breathe fire
They fly higher
If they had bad breathe
It could cause instant death.

Their scales look wet
They are hard I bet
The bigger their claws
The wider their jaws
With teeth so white
It can give you a fright
When they flap their wings
The sound just rings.

Jamie Saunders (12)
Ifield Community College

Opinion

One day during a very hot summer
On a carriage
Packed with people
There was a tramp on one side
And on the other side was a businessman
One side was a set of eyes
On the other side was a set of eyes
Through one side eyes sees a man
Trapped
His suit crushes him with
Pressures of life
Through the other set of eyes
He sees escape and freedom
Who's the wealthiest?

Stephan Mabley (14)
Ifield Community College

Tell Me A Lie

(Dedicated to Laura Cox)

I've known you all my life,
At least that's how it seems,
Never known another way,
Of living out a dream.

Now I know you're leaving me
And I'll never understand,
Before I let you walk away,
I have one last demand.

Tell me a lie
And say that you won't go,
Look in my eyes
And hold me even though.

I realise
You have to walk away
No more
Yesterday.

You always were my angel
Flying high above
Always looking out for me
The angel that I love.

Now my dreams are fading,
Like age old photographs,
They hurt too much to look at now,
Reminders of our past.

Tell me a lie
And say that you won't go
Look in my eyes
And hold me even though.

I realise
You have to walk away
No more
Yesterday.

Maybe we could stay together,
Maybe it could last forever,
Maybe if you just tell me a lie,
Maybe then we'll never say goodbye.

David Ross Pollard (15)
Ifield Community College

Hallowe'en

Tonight is trick or treating,
Everybody will be out,
Collecting a trick or a treat,
Dressing up as a witch or
Vampire, maybe a ghost!
Children knocking on doors,
Adults giving out candy,
All this for three words,
Trick or treat!
They are having fun,
Laughing and joking,
Knocking on every door,
As they go through the
Neighbourhood,
Collecting sweets and tricks
From every door,
But some adults don't give,
On their door, they have a sign
Saying,
No trick or treaters
Then the fun is at home,
Stuffing and scoffing
Their faces with the sweets
They collected.

Carna Humphries (14)
Ifield Community College

Dragons' World

When walking through the forest one day,
I saw a dragon pass my way,
He said 'Hello' and then 'Goodbye,'
And wandered back to his dragon time.

And that very night, I ran away to find
The dragon I saw earlier that day
I went to the forest and climbed the highest tree
But I still couldn't find the dragon who was so polite to me.

I was upset,
I started to cry,
I wanted that dragon back here by my side.

That very next day the dragon came back,
He was a friendly nice dragon
But I had to except the fact
The dragon couldn't stay here,
Where would he go?
But he can still come today and
Again tomorrow.

Fenella Riley (12)
Ifield Community College

Dragon's Rage

In the darkest cave
Where the walls burst into flames
A dragon does fight
A restless knight
The sword slices
And the flames burn
But only one will return.

Lee Warren (12)
Ifield Community College

Dragon

A tall strong creature
Monster at work
A villain in the distance,
Also can breathe fire.

It swoops from left to right
Opens up its huge wings
Swoops down to grab its prey.

I caught a person, a man
The man screamed and shouted
Fighting for his life.

The creature was too strong and defeats the man
Then in a minute the thing flies back to its cave
Gone to sleep like nothing happened.

What is it? It's a dragon.

Daley Oladapo (13)
Ifield Community College

What Am I? (Unicorn)

I am beautiful and elegant,
As swift as a hawk,
My blood is as pure as an angels
And if anyone was to see me,
They would surely talk!

You will only see me in fairy tales
And I always leave circular trails,
I have a long shiny horn,
Yep, you got it, I'm a unicorn.

Ben Kinloch (12)
Ifield Community College

The Things I Hate About You

I hate the way you look at me,
I hate it when you talk,
I hate it when you stop and stare,
I hate the way you walk.

I hate the way you drink your tea,
I hate your stupid shirts,
I hate the way you shout at me
And how you think I'm dirt.

I hate the way you tell your jokes
And how you're really tall,
I hate the way I don't hate you,
Not even a bit,
Not even at all.

Kimberley Jones (13)
Ifield Community College

The Dragon

Dragons are creatures who like to breathe fire
They like to fly higher and higher and higher
They're nice to look at and nice to see
Then one day the dragon breathes.

I like dragons, especially nice ones,
Colourful and baby ones,
The dragon's cave is dark and gloomy
He hates to see the sunlight funny.

One day the dragon came out
And then he goes on a walkabout
He doesn't go far but goes away
And then he never comes back to find his prey.

Christopher Dunning (12)
Ifield Community College

My Poem

A black hole
A circle of defeat
A sign of anger
A purple heart.

A mark of an enemy
A ring full of hate
How many can one
Person take?

A purple flower
A sign of power
A firework of colours
A field of poppies.

A painful experience
A limited time only
A blue and purple puddle
A rainbow ripple.

What am I . . . ?

Damaris Jarman (13)
Ifield Community College

Me And Him

My life is like a cloud,
It can be all soft and fluffy,
But when the rain sets in,
My feelings drip on out.

I'm in love with a person,
Who's tender and kind,
He can be just like my cloud,
But I can never tell him aloud.

Sydney Watts (13)
Ifield Community College

City Kid

*(For a city kid in a country village who wakes up remembering the sights,
sounds and smells of the city)*

Dawn breaks
the city kid starts to wake up and come to his senses
he remembers the roar of the main road
the shouts from below
but in reality it's totally different
it's totally different.

For what the city kid really heard when he was awoken
was nothing but the sound of the sun shining
and the birds soaring
because that is his reality, that is his reality
even though he doesn't want it to be.

The city kid looks out of the window
he sees the invisible trucks, cars, people, large buildings
and grey, grey clouds above
but that's not what he really sees because in reality
                        it's totally different,
it's totally different.

For what the city kid really saw when he looked out the window
was a sea of bright green
and a desert of hay stacks
because that is his reality, that is his reality
even though he doesn't want it to be.

The city kid sits up and smells the smells that are outside
he smells the shinny oil, the grey cloudy smoke from the large trucks
the smell of cigarette smoke and the hint of alcohol in the air
but that's not what he really smells because in reality
                        it's totally different
it's totally different.

For what the city kid really smelt outside
was the clean, fresh air, the flowery ground
and the hint of manure
because that is his reality, that is his reality
even though he doesn't want it to be.

The city kid really wants to be back in the city
with the good old sounds, sights and smells
not in the countryside where it was totally different.
The kid wants to be a city kid again
A city kid again.

Chris Sinclair (14)
Ifield Community College

Hallowe'en

Tonight is for trick or treating,
Everybody will be out,
Collecting a trick or a treat,
Dressing up as a witch or vampire,
Or maybe even a ghost!
Children knocking on doors,
Adults giving out candy,
All this for three words,
Trick or treat!
They are having fun,
Laughing and joking,
Knocking on every door,
As they go through the
Neighbourhood
Collecting sweets from door to door,
Who could ask for any more?
Everyone is having fun,
Until they come to the door with the note that
Says:
'No trick or treaters!'

Nicola Barton (13)
Ifield Community College

Tornado

A spiral,
A cloud of dust,
A giant Hoover,

Somewhere over the rainbow,
It's like the hand of God,
Reaching down and taking away tiny buildings.

A giant cloud of grey that
Casts a shadow over the
Terrified town below it.

Finally it touches down
Ripping everything in
Its path,
Leaving a trail of destruction
Behind it.

Luke Foster (13)
Ifield Community College

Metaphor Poem

G iant rare sea creatures,
U nderstood by few,
E stimated to become extinct,
S ome are still out there,
S ea is home.

W ill the species continue to survive?
H abitat for most is in enclosures,
A cross between a whale and a sealion,
T ime is nearly up for the
Manatee!

Nicole Jarosinski (13)
Ifield Community College

Anger

I stand here, normal, waiting,
A sudden flash of movement, light,
Anger, hate, evil pulsates
No one knows the damage that was done.

His pride takes a beating,
The verbal abuse
But he deserves it
Never again will he anger me.

But now is all worse
He cowers in fear, his actions don't show it
But his eyes show all,
Yet no one but me can see it.

Again the inside flashes out,
Fast as light, grabs the neck,
Throttles, throttles
Then regains what is his, the outer shell regained.

People's pride takes beatings
For I let my guard down
But no remorse is there,
Yet only hate is there.

Ian Brown (15)
Ifield Community College

Metaphor Poem

I'm a stone, I'm a story and a book,
I'm an ally and an enemy but I cannot cook.

I'm a statue, I'm a rock and time will never see,
Another thing that can cope like me.

I'm a devil, I'm an angel, I'm a group,
I'm a thing that things can eat just like soup.

I'm part of a job, I'm a big, ugly and old thing,
I'm a thing with no brain and I cannot sing.

I'm a lion, I'm a tiger but I cannot kill,
I'm an ugly thing that will never be ill.

I'm the wind, I'm the rain and I'm turned into stairs,
I'm always about when hunted in pairs.

I'm a little bigger than England and tied up in vines,
I'm a thing that has no straight lines.

Adam Hunn (13)
Ifield Community College

When You Went

The silence of the room when you went was like as
                                    dead as night.
The way you used to kiss my lips was like we
                were the only people left in the world.
The letters you used to write me would explain the way you feel.
The birds that used to sing in the trees when you would
                                    make morning coffee.
The way you used to lay beside me and cuddle my tears away.
Now that this has all gone, I can't take it in.
But I believe you are still here and that your spirit will never
Leave my side and one day we will be joined and spend all the time we
Have lying in the clouds singing our beloved song.

Gemma Higgins (14)
Ifield Community College

Where Did We Come From?

Did we come from the sky?
Did we come from the ground?
Did we come from the sea?
Did we come from the trees?
If we didn't come from any of these, where did we come from?
Did we come from a meteor smashing into Earth?
Did we come from the sun exploding?
Did we come from a computer?
Did we come from Mars or Jupiter?
If we didn't come from any of these, how do we exist?
Did we come from a cupboard?
Did we come from the moon?
Did we come from a pen?
Did we come from a shop?
If we didn't come from any of these, were we just put here?

Eiblisha Taylor & Sharna Evans (13)
Ifield Community College

The Dragon

D angerous like a lion with a sore head,
R aging like a bat out of hell,
A nnoyed with the huntsman who now is dead,
G raceful like a fish in the sea,
O range like a flower lying in a flowerbed,
N ever to be seen again.

Shaunie Chisling (13)
Ifield Community College

About A Little Girl

The children play all dressed in weird clothes,
The trees are swaying as the wind blows,
The day was here but the night now falls,
The cloud comes over, the rain starts to fall.
People are running so they don't get wet,
But one little girl is all alone standing in the
Middle of the road, she sees a light coming
From up the road,
Out steps a lady with her arm in the air,
The girl gasps for air - the rain gets harder,
She starts to cry, it was her mum.
With her arms in the air
Now the little girl is safe and now
Thank God that love is all that she's blessed with,
Everyone's love.

Joanne Moule (15)
Ifield Community College

The Clean, The Dirty

Two rich people in a Mercedes car
Staring at the dustmen looking poor as they are.
While they sit at the lights and wait thinking
The dustmen looking a state.
Feeling elegant, smart and clean,
The dustmen stare back strong and mean.

James Pearl (14)
Ifield Community College

My Weekend

An alarm is ringing and I hear a sound,
I must get up to do my paper round,
It's 6.45 and I'm off on my bike
Soon back for some breakfast to have something I like.

No school today, but I don't frown,
I've collected my wages and I'm off to town,
I think I might buy a new CD,
Or maybe a camera that I might see.

Later, I'm off to the park,
For a game of football or a bit of a lark,
This evening to the cinema I might be going,
I'll check the local newspaper to see what's showing.

On Sunday I'm going for a ride on my bike,
Then home to do some homework, which I dislike,
It's Sunday evening, the weekend is done,
Back to school on Monday - that's not fun!

James Foster (13)
Ifield Community College

My Dragon

I had a dragon
Which blew lots of fire
It had a green stripy back
And flew for lots of days.

I have a dragon
He's bold and green
When he comes out to play
He makes my life gleam.

He's nice and gentle
When he blows his fire
But beware he can't
Balance on a wire.

Ryan Ellery (12)
Ifield Community College

A Shining Light

A shining light all through day
You know by night it'll go away
A bright big bulb in the supper sky
It will live forever and never die.

A shining light that is so bright
It likes to hide all through the night
His beautiful rays are so very great
In the morning he is never late.

A shining light in a ball of fire
To give off light is his one desire
He asks himself 'What am I?'
He is the light that will never die.

Stephen Thompson (13)
Ifield Community College

I Hate The Way You . . .

I hate the way you don't tell jokes,
I hate the way your voice just croaks,
I hate the way you stand and stare,
I hate the way you just don't care.

I hate the way you drink your drink,
I hate the way you really stink,
I hate the way you stuff your face,
I hate the way you think it's a race.

I hate the way you walk about,
I hate the way you scream and shout,
I hate the way you brush your hair,
You really are a nightmare!

Simone Harris (13)
Ifield Community College

Harvest From An Asian Point Of View

No harvest for us, nothing is grown,
Although the seeds were properly sown.
No food for us to gather in,
Nothing to eat, we just get thin.
Those monsoon rains have come again,
Destroyed our crops and caused our pain.
They take the goodness from the soil
And ruin the farmers labour and toil.
The blazing sun, we get all year,
A little rain would be the cure,
But June to October, with torrential rain,
Can grow our crops or cause us pain.
Wheat, millet, rice, cotton and tea
We are the biggest producers you'll ever see.
But not this year, as you now know,
Because this year they fail to grow.
In the western world it must be great,
To sit at the table and fill your plate,
To fill the churches with all that food,
When our places of worship just sit nude.
To sing praises to our God above,
When food to eat is what we love.
We have no crops to store all year round,
Just hunger and starvation to be found.
So think of us when you feed the unfortunate few,
Our large country could do with help from you,
With irrigation and modern ideas.

We'll soon be rid of all our fears.

Nicholas O'Leary (10)
Michael Ayres Junior School

School Bully!

I don't know why they do it,
I don't do anything to them,
I am always good at home
And my mum thinks I'm a gem!

They're always cheating in tests,
It really is not fair,
So I am proud of myself
And frankly I don't care!

I really hate gym
And I'm really, really slow,
They always get on the apparatus,
I think I should have a go!

I like being kind,
I get lots and lots of friends,
If they want me to be a bully
It will have to depend!

Lana Brooker (12)
Millais School

The Shark

I am going to tell you about a shark,
They come in all sorts of shapes and sizes, light or dark,
He swims around
Without a sound.
With two eyes that are bright,
They shine at midnight.
With teeth like diamonds
That stick out like daggers.
He's slippery,
He's slimy,
He's deadly, he's mad
And his manners are bad.

Sarah Jane Coxall (12)
Millais School

Misty Moon

As the misty moon dwells on us, he reflects on the sparkling lake
as it ripples across the surface.
I start to wonder if he really has light, or does he steal it from the sun?
But does it matter? For he does not make the human run,
or the first morning bird sing.
He shelters the creatures of the night;
The bloodthirsty fox as he hunts for the rabbit,
The wise owl flying in the night sky
And the grey wolf as he howls to him.
He inspires evil like the old hag, who is far from anything civilised;
she is rumoured to be a witch!
The pale vampire in his tomb
And the evil spirit that brings water to our hearts.
We rely on shining sun to bring us light,
She can honestly say that light is hers.
As for the moon, is he really trustworthy?
I don't know, we don't even know where he comes from,
For he does not rise and set like the sun,
He is always up there, waiting to take over,
So next time it is day, see if you can see him waiting.

Elspeth Waters Brown (11)
Millais School

Town

Every Saturday we go down town,
We like to shop and mess around.
We try on shoes in all the shops,
Then we like to look at tops.

We go to McDonald's to eat our meals,
Then we go to the cinema to watch some films.
We go to Costa Coffee to get some drinks,
Then we catch the bus home and say our goodbyes.
We can't wait till Monday to say our hi's.

Megan Haney (12)
Millais School

The A To Z Of . . .

A is for apples, juicy and sweet.
B is for bats, who like to eat meat.
C is for cats, who lie around and take naps!
D is for donkeys, who wear New York caps.
E is for eggs, scrambled, poached or fried.
F is for frogs, when they left their mother cried!
G is for giraffes, they can see over roofs.
H is for horses, who have big hooves!
I is for ignoring, when someone won't talk.
J is for Jerusalem, where Jesus once walked.
K is for kicking karate, 'Ha-ya!'
L is for litter, if you drop it a-ha!
M is for Monday, we really don't like it!
N is for noise, cello, flute and drum kit.
O is for octopus, eight long legs.
P is for people, eating boiled eggs!
Q is for quadrilateral, rectangles and squares.
R is for rare; tiger, elephants and bears.
S is for silence, it doesn't stay for long!
T is for trouble, everything is wrong.
U is for ultimate, when you reach the top.
V is for vultures, who fly and can't stop!
W is for wasps, you'll get a nasty sting!
X is for xylophone, with a ring, ting, ting!
Y is for yellow, colourful and bright.
Z is for zombie, it'll give you a fright.

Megan Whitty (11)
Millais School

A To Z Of Names

A is for Amy who always jumps.
B is for Ben who has lots of lumps.
C is for Charlotte who is always on a swing.
D is for Denim who's worth more than a pound.
E is for Ella who's always round.
F is for Fred who loves to have some drink.
G is for Georgina whose favourite colour is pink.
H is for Hannah who loves to play on the slide.
I is for Isabella who likes to hide.
J is for Jessica who is really cool.
K is for Kelsey who has a big pool.
L is for Leighton who always lies.
M is for Megan whose pets die.
N is for Nikky who Mum always bites.
O is for Oliver who is always in a fight.
P is for Pia who likes to lay on the beach.
Q is for Quarmie who is always eating a peach.
R is for Rebecca who likes to teach.
S is for Shirstin who likes to be taught.
T is for Tristan who was often in court.
U is for Urica who was a bit of a sleeker.
V is for Viv who was a bit of a streaker.
W is for William who is nice and kind.
X is for Xavier who has a clever mind.
Y is for Yasim who did a poo.
Z is for Zoe who was always on the loo.

Kelsey Baldock (11)
Millais School

My Trip To Dubai!

The hot sun landing on the crystal clear salt sea spray,
people lying in natural beauty
on tiny grains of sand.

Children splashing in and out
of the pool, the laughs, the giggles,
the screams, the shouts.

Jet skis shooting along the spicy sea.
Shoals of fish swimming on by.
Bright colours flashing before your very eyes.

In the gold souk, diamond,
rubies, real and fake,
shop assistants' smiles make you feel great.

Bump, bump, bump along the dunes
and a snake slithering on past
and the sun setting in the west.

And that's a day in the life of Dubai.

Olivia Barnett (12)
Millais School

My Dream Boy!

My dream boy is sort of tall,
Completely cool but that's not all.
He likes school a little bit,
Not a geek with a zit.

He has brownish eyes that shimmer in the light,
Be careful they could give you a fright.
My dream boy is very pretty,
Sometimes I take the mickey.

My dream boy is very cute,
I think he might play the flute!

Chantal Range (13)
Millais School

The Night Star

I glanced out of my window
And my eye was caught.
There was something
That shone
And twinkled
In my eye.
I looked a bit harder,
What did I see?
The most beautiful star
Sparkling in many different colours
And a million different shades.
It stood out
From all the other stars.
I had a dream that night
And wondered
If I would ever see
That amazing
Star again.

Chloe Crellin (11)
Millais School

A Lovely Time

One dark foggy night
At midnight
Two animals were having a fight.
One minute it was midnight,
The next sunny dawn.
All peaceful and quiet
The children would play at midday.
The adults would chit-chat,
What a lovely day.

Kimberley Barker (11)
Millais School

Autumn Has Begun

I looked out my window summer has gone,
Making me think Christmas won't be long.
The autumn leaves are falling,
Orange and red all around.
The squirrels they are digging,
Burying food all around.

All the birds are leaving,
Heading south to the sun.
The mornings are now crisper,
When will snow arrive?

Snow has arrived,
Only one day to go,
Closer and closer it gets
For Santa to arrive.

Ella Bussey (11)
Millais School

Flowers

Flowers are bright like the sun,
Their colours stand out
And never fade away.

The stem so green
With sap running down it,
All of the petals joint to it,
With a few leaves attached.

Seeds make flowers
With water and plant food,
The roots are what keep it together,
Flowers are beautiful.

Chelsea Draisey (11)
Millais School

Rabbits

Rabbits have big ears
a twitchy nose
and little toes
fluffy tails
and big eyes
they skip and bound
along the ground
under the ground
they dig a warren
and lining a nest with fur
for babies due in spring
in the spring the babies come
and soon they'll bounce and play around.

Hannah Norris (12)
Millais School

The Lake

Here I stand with the wind blowing in my hair,
The leaves fall in the lake,
As the lake shimmers I see beautiful nature,
As I look over the other side,
Deer are sipping from the water,
Rabbits are leaping over logs to my side
And to my other side are sheep in the field,
As I look around I see lots of bridges,
I cross one and sit on the river bank
I see ducks and fish,
Nobody's around, it is calm on the landscape,
A breathtaking view, that's so peaceful,
Just how you would picture in a perfect dream!

Chloe Gladwish (11)
Millais School

My Kitten

My kitten, he is wacky and really, really mad,
He jumps around like a rabbit, and is never ever sad.
He likes to chase his tail, round and round and round,
But when he gets tired, he flops down on the ground.

My kitten, who is weird, is a bit like a dog,
And as he's only little, he will sleep like a log.
If he jumps at you, he will give you quite a shock,
But don't take your shoes off, or he will chew your sock.

He'll wipe his food bowl clean if there's any food,
And he'll eat anything, whether it's bitten, or chewed.
But when it's time for bed, and night-time is drawing,
He doesn't really care, as he'll do it in the morning!

I love my kitten so much, I'm really glad he's mine,
I love my family just as much, and in my heart he'll always shine.

Josie Nelder (11)
Millais School

Sound, Smell And Taste!

That horrible, horrible sound,
The sound of a scratch on an old blackboard,
The squeak of a high-pitched note in music,
The squeal of a very loud scream.

That horrible, horrible smell,
The smell of burnt bread just out of the toaster,
The smell of root beer in your cup,
The smell of people's armpits.

That horrible, horrible taste,
The taste of sour apples,
The taste of tangy tomatoes,
The taste of dry chicken grinding in your mouth.

Emily Smith (11)
Millais School

The Boy

Can you see that boy in the corner?
All alone
He's always there, it's almost as if that's his home
He hardly ever moves, with his eyes wide and pale face
It seems like he's in a world of his own,
Gazing into nowhere.
I wonder what life is like through his eyes
No family, no friends,
Just a photo to remind him of those he loves.
Where had they gone?
I can't imagine what it would be like to be out there on my own.
Day and night passers-by looking at me,
Like I'm nothing
He's so quiet, he's only seven
I live across the road to where's he's staying
Some nights I hear him crying in his sleep, reaching out for his mum
I can't understand why this is happening.
Tonight I see a car pull up next to him, a lady runs up to him crying.
He shouts out something . . .
'Mummy!'
The lady picks him up crying, laughing, screaming, 'My baby!'
She hugs him, he kisses her back
She puts him down,
Still crying,
She takes his hand,
'You're coming home!'
She kisses him then they drive off.
This morning I'm reading the news
'Boy reunited with mother after 1 year'
And there I see for the first time in 1 year,
That boy in the corner, smiling.

Catrin Williams (11)
Millais School

Flying

Flying is making your dreams all come true
You spread your wings and fly higher than life!

Flying is believing beyond the clouds
Catching breeze in your face and wind in your hair!

Flying is being on top of the world
You're king of the sky!

Flying is making friends with the birds
Floating in mid-air watching the ground!

Flying is taking the time to be you
Finding your soul up in the air!

Flying is having a mind of your own
Passing through clouds listening for no sound!

I could fly for a lifetime, fly for a year
I don't want to stop this fantasy so big!

Rachel Pearson (11)
Millais School

Best Friend

B est friend
E very day
S miling always
T rue as she can be.

F riends forever
R emember the good times together
I listen to her every day
E very word means a lot to me
N o one could replace her!
D iamond, she's a true gem!

Rachel Banks (12)
Millais School

About A Tramp

It's cold and I'm old
And I live on my own
On a bench which is hard and numb.
I am poor, homeless,
Hungry and tired
I sit on the streets begging for money
All I think about is my hungry tummy.

Some people think I'm unbearable
Some people think I stink
Some people think I'm horrible
I don't care what people think!

I live on people's waste
The taste is very bland.
Food they throw away in haste
But to me it tastes grand.

The last strings of my dignity
Were ripped from me when
I had to leave my home and sleep on the streets.

I'm all alone and live on my own
I'm lonely, sad but that's too bad
Because this is my life till it mends.

Charlotte Bearman (12)
Millais School

Wild Stallions

Wild stallions galloping
Through the wild wind
Blowing and whistling
Throwing their manes and tails.

They're like speeding eagles
Going over the plains.
The wind getting wilder and wilder
By the minute.

They come to a halt
With a buck and a rear.
The wind has stopped
Its wildness.

The stallions start,
Now they become wild again.
Stallions start to shake their heads
Do small rears, there in the trees,
Leaves going side to side,
Up and down.
Then the wild stallions stop and go.

Jessica Munden (13)
Millais School

Winter

I am the chill that sneaks down your coat.
I am the sharp breeze that makes your nose cold.
I am the dew on a frosty morning.
I am the snow that seeps through your gloves.
I am the wind that makes the leaves dance.
I am the howling that keeps you awake.
I am, I am winter.

Catherine Tingley (11)
Millais School

A Bowl Of Fruit

A huge, yellow, patterned bowl,
Standing on its own, on the walnut table,
Fruit all laid neatly in the bowl,
A glorious sight, a bowl of fruit.

Big, round, blood-red oranges shimmering in the sunlight,
Bendy, yellow, squishy bananas waiting to be eaten,
Scratchy, hairy, green kiwi fruit over ripe waiting to be peeled,
A glorious sight, a bowl of fruit.

Rosy-red, glossy, crunchy apples munch, munch, munch,
Small, sour, oval grapes bursting with juice,
Yellow, tasty melons full of seeds,
A glorious sight, a bowl of fruit.

Green, hard, long stalked pears rocking to and fro,
Hard, brown coconuts, milk swishing inside them,
Children grabbing their piece of fruit, munching on it,
A glorious sight, a bowl of fruit.

Gemma McKale (11)
Millais School

My Favourite Things

Freshly cut grass when my dad's just mowed the lawn,
The juicy, yellow taste and smell of just cooked corn,
The freezing feel of soaking wet ice,
The sound of thunder as it gives me a fright,
Rough sandpaper making indents in my hand,
The boiling, golden grains of sand,
I love the smell of my old school,
I love the smell of my best friend's pool,
I love the smell of hot apple pie,
The sight of a bird that's just flown by.
Lilies scattered on a stream's coast,
But the warm smell of horses I love the most.

Rachael Holding (11)
Millais School

Green Dragon

I saw a great green dragon
Standing by a stream
With bright gold wings
Which shimmered in the breeze

In the moonlight that shone in the valley
Twinkling above the dragon's lair
He stood in deep fear
As the human raised his almighty sword

With one great whoosh
The human took his first swipe of victory
But it wasn't over yet
The dragon rose up and with one spear of fire
Struck the human down

May he rest in peace.

Emma Farnes (11)
Millais School

Worst Things

I hate zooming motorbikes whizzing past,
Wiggling spiders running fast.
Jellied cat food brown and cold,
Smelly bananas, mushy and old.
Lonely dogs howling in the night,
I hate powdery white chalk, scratchy light.
Loud vacuum twisting and turning,
Waiting for lunch with my stomach churning.
Dry mud under my nails,
I hate rough leathery crocodile tails.
Also horrible long wigs
Stepping on twigs.
Strong, fiery, yellow mustard,
I hate shampoo in my mouth, thick like custard,
These are some of my worst things.

Lauren Fuller (11)
Millais School

Millais School

Millais is funky and fun
with nice teachers and friends
the only problem is I keep
getting lost round all the bends.

The canteen has gorgeous food
with cherry tart and iced buns
but my favourite has to be
by far the best, muffin Friday fun.

Hockey is my worst sport
as I don't know how to play,
but guess what I'm form captain
lucky me, oh hey.

Now it's the end of school
time to say goodbye
I'm going home now
cheerio, bye-bye.

Megan Evans (11)
Millais School

Angel

Her eyes are glistening like shiny topaz stones
Her halo is like a brand new wedding ring,
Gold and twinkling in the sun
Her dress is like a fresh patch of clean snow,
Whiter than white,
Her wings as light as candyfloss
Floating and whipping the air ever so gently
She looks like a million pounds.

Gemma Rivers (11)
Millais School

Favourite Things

A calm river flowing through the countryside
My guinea pig's squeak coming from behind
The lovely smell of a red rose
Drifting swiftly past my nose.
The smooth stones from Cornwall's best beach
A beautiful, soft, juicy, ripe peach,
The sight of a sunset on the water's edge,
Whooshing down the snowy hill on my bright pink sledge
Some cooked chips straight from the chippy
The taste of Walls' Cornetto Whippy.
The smell of petrol as we sit in the station
The roller coaster ride is a thrilling sensation
Fireworks on a crisp, cold night
A windy autumn day flying my kite
These are a few of my favourite things!

Laura Drew (11)
Millais School

Flash Of Light

The rain had licked the pavement overnight,
So you could see the shining light,
Through a crack in the wall,
It seemed so small,
Disappeared in a flash,
Followed by a crash,
I crept cautiously to see what was there,
There was no one,
No one at all.

Charlotte Perrelle (11)
Millais School

Worst Things

The touch of chalk makes me cringe,
The noise of a baby starting to whinge,
The smell of marzipan straight from the packet,
The noise of a ball hitting a racquet,
The taste of cheese and onion crisps
And also Mum's Brussel sprouts burnt to a crisp,
The sight of stinky, scurrying rats,
The sound of fighting cats,
The smell of smoke from a burning fire
The noise of a skid from a tyre,
Animal testing makes me mad,
Screaming children makes me sad,
The smell of mouldy cheese straight from the fridge,
Big hairy spiders sitting on a ridge,
Those are a few of my worst things.

Katie Harding (11)
Millais School

The Sea

I close my eyes
as the sea flows up to my toes
the seagulls fly above
then the water goes

The sea is like a lion pouncing
for its prey
I look above at the sky
and think what a lovely day

In the distance the whales
swim in the sea
the breeze blows against my face.
It's lovely being at the beach
with no one else . . . just me!

Georgia Gregory (11)
Millais School

A Robin

A red breasted robin,
Sitting in a hedge,
It's little head a-noddin',
To its babies on the ledge!

A red breasted robin,
Sitting in a tree,
Its little head a-bobbin',
To the chirping melody!

A red breasted robin,
Flying in the sky,
Its children are a-snoozin',
And she's gliding up so high!

A red breasted robin,
Coming home to rest,
Her babies are a-snorin',
As they snuggle in the nest!

A red breasted robin,
Like the calm after the storm,
Her babies are a-wakin',
For the coming of the dawn!

Amanda Gilbert (11)
Millais School

Favourite Things

The delightful smell of freshly baked bread,
As I the zombie surfaces from bed.

Wonderful Cadbury's chocolate secretly swallowed,
And horror movies with someone being followed.

Tickling my feet as I walk on warm sand in Spain,
But once I return to England all there is, is rain.

Football roaring as England are world winners,
Granny's yummy roast dinners.

Twist, turn, whizz, woz on a roller coaster,
My favourite David Beckham poster.

Banana split mixed with jelly,
Whilst watching EastEnders on telly.

The bell that goes at the end of the day,
As I walk home from Millais.

Don't forget my golden rings,
These are all my favourite things.

Ashleigh Bayton (11)
Millais School

The Black Swan

The snapping of their beaks
As they fly across peaks
Gracefully flying
With no fear of dying
They fly over towns
Waiting to drift down
As their beaks stand out like the sun
They are waiting and waiting
For their flight to be done.

Sarah Kitchen (11)
Millais School

Bad Things

I hate the cold and the rain,
I really wished I lived in Spain.

Seeing animals in a cage,
That really makes me want to rage.

I hate the frost and the ice,
Unless it's in a drink that's nice.

I hate going to bed early
Or when my hair goes curly.

I hate car fumes
And some perfumes.

I hate it when people smoke,
Because it makes people choke.

I hate spiders and other bugs
But I love big fat pugs.

I hate the sound of the dentist drill
Or when I am feeling ill.

I hate mustard
And runny custard.

But the one thing I hate the most is when
I get my mobile phone bill through the post.

Charlotte Harris (11)
Millais School

My Favourite Things

I love the smell of my grandma's washing machine soap
It never makes me mope.
I adore to stroke my small cat,
She doesn't like to sleep upon a mat.
I like to poke squidgy jelly,
While I watch the telly.
I love to eat cake mix,
While the clock ticks.
I adore the taste of Chinese food,
While my sister is being rude.
I love to hear the rain,
When I come back from Spain.
I love the sound of birds tweeting,
I forgot what friend I'm supposed to be meeting.
I adore the sound of the sea on the shore,
While I chuck my apple core.
I like the look of Malham Cove,
My favourite colour is mauve.
Also the look of the countryside,
With my sister by my side.
Not forgetting my golden rings,
These are a few of my favourite things.

Vanessa Robinson Caturla (11)
Millais School

My Favourite Things

I love to stroke my dog,
Her soft fur on my hand,
I also love the Horsham band
And my gerbil scurrying
Across my hand,
I love lying on the sand,
I like the sound of the waves
Crashing on the rocks,
When I'm in my bright
Pink and orange socks,
I like to touch snow,
Seeing it glisten on my gloves,
My brother is the best of brovs,
I like to eat jelly
Whilst watching the telly,
I love playing the flute,
Whilst in my black boots,
Lilies, how I love the smell,
And the 3 o'clock bell,
These are some of my favourite things,
And I like it when my sister sings.

Lara Hutchison (11)
Millais School

I Look Out My Window

I look out my window and see . . .
Trees, houses, cars and people
But no sound.

I look out my window and see . . .
The wind blowing the trees from side to side
I see the lights turning on and off in the houses
The cars flying past and the people walking.
But no sound.

I look out my window and see . . .
The squirrels climbing up the tree to get to their nuts
The houses with the curtains shut
And the people stepping step by step by step
But no sound.

I look out my window and see . . .
The leaves falling from the autumn trees
And the houses stay as still as a statue
I see the cars crushing the leaves that had settled on the road
And the people's hair covering up their faces from the subtle wind.
But no sound.

I look out my window and hear nothing!

Beth Wrigley (11)
Millais School

Seasons

Frozen lakes and icy streams
Misty morning, winter dreams.
Building snowmen piece by piece
Roasting turkey, Christmas feast.

Winter melting into spring
New flowers grow, birds start to sing.
Lambs are born and dance around
Listen to the new spring sound.

The sun comes out to warm the air
Barbecues and summer fayre.
Holiday bags are packed to go
School is out and faces glow.

Twirling, swirling, falling leaves
Autumn wind blows through the trees.
This is where my seasons end
But then again winter's round the bend.

Lauren Law (11)
Millais School

Snowflakes

Snowflakes drop, here and there
They hop to and fro, twinkling in the air.
The cool winter's breeze blows in my face,
So I start to run at a medium pace.
I watch the snowflakes land on the ground.
They're very quiet and don't make a sound.
All these people playing in the snow
While I sit down, hiding low.
I wish snow didn't go away
When snow's here it's always a happy day.

Francesca Smith (11)
Millais School

King Of The Jungle

The mighty creature strong and proud
Laying down on the satin rug
No shaggy fur
Not a bit of dirt
He is so fierce yet he appears so calm
His golden coat worn with pride
His head up high
No room for shame
The well groomed mane that sits round his neck
Makes him look so soft not tough one bit
But when the danger strikes nearby
He is alert, running faster than light
The scare has passed
And so he returns
To sit upon the glistening throne
The noise dies down
He rests his eyes
And so there lies . . .
The king of the jungle!

Hollie Cousins (11)
Millais School

Snowflakes

Snowflakes are born in the clouds,
Like bubbles being blown gently into the sky.
When the time is right, the clouds drop their heavy load
And the snowflakes, gently flutter to the ground.
When the sun rises and shines on the fluffy snowflakes
They glitter like diamonds.
When the sun rises even more,
The fluffy snowflakes disappear into the mist,
Never to be found again.

Mary-Anne Frank (12)
Millais School

If I Had Wings

If I had wings,
    I would taste a chunk of the burning sun.

If I had wings,
    I would smell the sweet scent of the rainbow.

If I had wings,
    I would listen to the song of the nightingale
    The song no other creature can sing.

If I had wings,
    I would gaze at the angels floating in mid air.

If I had wings,
    I would touch the ice cream clouds as cold as ice.

If I had wings,
    I would dream of flying with Pegasus
    And walking the rainbow.

Chloe Loader (12)
Millais School

Winter Has Come

Autumn has passed,
Winter creeps upon us,
The wind starts to howl like a wolf calling for its cubs,
The snow falls like leaves dropping from a tree,
As everyone wraps up warm,
Animals begin to hibernate,
Children throw snowballs as they think of Christmas,
All creatures look forward to spring
For it is a new beginning.

Gemma Humphreys (11)
Millais School

Me

My mum, my dad, my sisters too,
All the things that we all do.
The park, on holiday and on the beach,
My family are always in reach.
Baked beans are my deadly sins,
I just get through tins and tins.
Snow before it totally melts,
Bright orange and yellow belts.
The giant monster under my bed,
The little noises in my head.
A great big elephant with cute, big eyes,
I've even seen one that flies.
But I hope you see
This is just me,
Me, me, me, me!

Sophie Goodwin (11)
Millais School

Good And Bad

My food is a winner
Unlike food for dinner
My cat is fluffy
Unlike the dog who's scruffy
My cousin will be wed
But I want my bed
I love my telly
And love my jelly
My friend is moaning
I'm just groaning
I like pop
My mum says I should stop.

I'm fed up
I'm going to bed!

Becky Robins (11)
Millais School

Monday Mornings

My alarm clock rings at twenty to seven,
Not one of the joys of being eleven!
Half an hour later I creep out of bed,
Just to jump back in, it's as cold as the dead!
I get downstairs at twenty past,
I've got just fives minutes; I'll have to be fast!
At twenty-five past there's a knock on the door,
I'm nowhere near ready, she's early I'm sure!
Waiting at the bus stop in the freezing cold,
I should have worn a coat just like I was told!
When the bus finally comes it's quarter of eight,
I'm numb all over from the long wait!
At the back of the bus it's as mad as a zoo,
I wish that I could sit there too!
At quarter past eight the bus pulls in,
I'm glad to be away from that deafening din!
I'm just 7ST when I walk through the door,
Not an individual, not me anymore.
First and second periods pass me by,
But I haven't been listening, my head's in the sky!
I go back to the form room at breaktime to eat,
Though it's early I'm dead on my feet!
Third period's maths, we're doing a test,
Fourth is English, we're writing in best.
Finally it's lunchtime, the end of the morning,
What a pity that this week is only just dawning!

Isobel Darcy (11)
Millais School

Musical Notes

Musical notes
And warm, woolly coats,
A man playing the flute,
Going *toot-e-toot-toot,*
My favourite sound,
I give him a pound
And on he plays,
Throughout the days
And I'll keep coming back,
Until he starts to lack,
If he carries on playing
His hands will start fraying,
One day he'll be gone,
But we would all have to move on,
But at this time,
The sound is as nice as lemon and lime,
So on he plays,
Throughout the days
And he carries on playing,
On and on and on.

Georgina Carr (11)
Millais School

Heightophobia

I am scared of heights
Like a balloon is nervous of a pin
Like a pencil is frightened of a sharpener
Like silence doesn't like noise
Like a sandcastle is jumpy about the tide
Like a tree is horrified at a woodpecker
Like a lawn is terrified of a lawnmower
Like noodles are uneasy about chopsticks
I am scared of heights.

Eleanor Martin (11)
Millais School

Flight

Flying fast,
Flying high,
Flying swiftly,
Flying by.

Over deserts,
Over seas,
Over mountains,
Over trees.

Feel the warmth,
Feel the breeze,
Feel the droplets,
Feel us freeze.

Hear the silence,
See the world.

Nicola Dexter (11)
Millais School

Favourite Things

Mum's kiss on a Friday night,
Waking up to a Saturday light
Going swimming with my friends,
Hoping it will never end,
The sweet smell of flowers,
Playing for hours,
Cuddling my sister,
Popping a blister,
Horror movies that make me scream,
Apple pie with whipped cream,
Watching TV,
Listening to CDs,
Jumping off a diving board,
Like a bird on the wing,
Those are a few of my favourite things.

Molly McLean (11)
Millais School

My Favourite Things

I have many favourite things like a bird in the sky,
A shopping spree, just Mum and me,
A whole week of EastEnders, a bucket of popcorn,
A packet of crisps, a drink of fizz,
These are some of my favourite things.

I have many favourite things like a warm dish of pasta,
A new lamb born in the spring,
A night in with a pizza and TV,
A rainbow on a dark, rainy day,
These are some of my favourite things.

I have many favourite things like a whale in the sea,
A summer holiday after a long school term,
A whole group of chatty friends,
A birthday or Christmas with my family,
These are some of my favourite things.

I have many more favourite things,
You'll need another day,
As my list of favourite things
Would go on forever,
But I wouldn't have all day.

Katie Hedger (11)
Millais School

My Favourite Things

Creamy chocolate, on my tongue melts
Pretty pictures made with paints and felts,
The smell of books, all new and white
Crackling bonfires on an icy night,
Cuddly, warm coats in the winter's cold
Rings and necklaces of silver and gold,
Many more wonderful things I could tell
But that would take a page more as well.

Rachel Parker (11)
Millais School

I Hate . . .

Tipp-Ex when it's gone all gloopy
When I'm sad and feeling gloomy
Scary, spooky, pitch-black woods
And dark objects that look like hoods
Only the light of an orb-like moon
Hoping that I find my way home soon
The strong vile smell of fresh cow pat
The angry hissing of a cat
The sight of helpless slugs
Creepy-crawlies, insects and bugs
Curry, it tastes so yucky
Me, out of bed my hair is so mucky
As I watch the telly, skinny, ill people stare back at me
If they saw me, they would think, *who is she?*
I loath fights and wars
And people who slam those doors.
Being all alone in complete silence
And all the violence
That just goes to show
That the world has some bad things, you know.

Kristine Bates (11)
Millais School

All About Women

W omen are stressful, sensitive and kind
O pen to friends, no secrets kept between them,
M en protect them and treat them royally,
E laborately dressed, made up to the nines,
N eatly presented and protective of their young.
   Is there a thing that a woman hasn't done?

Rebecca Mash (13)
Millais School

I Hate . . .

I hate the sight of my brother's bedroom
As it feels my heart with gloom

I hate the smell of teacakes and kippers
And my dad's granny slippers

I really detest the feel of dripping wet tissues
And my hundred and one magazine issues

I can't stand the sound of classic music
And the smell of freshly vomited sick

I really don't like the word 'school'
And the feeling of dog drool

I really can't stand the smell of chlorine
And my brother's hygiene

I hate the sound of polythene being scratched
And things being matched

Fruit scones are the worst
As is following a long, black hearse

Thunder and lightning
Makes my life frightening

My worst sport is hockey
Frankie Dettori my hated jockey

Now do you really know why
I hate all those things.

Laura Wallis (11)
Millais School

My Favourite Things

My mum's perfume as it fills the air,
Lavender roses as I sit on the garden chair.

The smell of petrol blocks my nose,
The smell of my body spray 'Pose'.

Home-made apple crumble,
Makes my tummy rumble.

Melted cheese on toast.
Nothing's better than a Sunday roast.

When the phone rings I wonder who it could be.
Someone knocks on the door, I hope it's someone for me.

The touch of fluffy dogs, I can't resist,
A balloon flying in the sky like it doesn't exist.

The sound of wind rushing past
When people say it's going to be sunny on the weather forecast.

When I see the sunset rising through the old oak tree,
When I go to the pier I look out to sea.

As the pine clock hands tinged,
I told you a few of my favourite things.

Lauren Bristow (11)
Millais School

Worst Things Poem

Going to the dentist, and listening to the drill,
Blood trickling down, and people feeling ill.
Children touching maggots so slimy and so small,
Jumping straight away in a freezing swimming pool.
Visiting the vets, putting creatures down,
The dry and scaly snakes coiling all around.
Walking through a floor shop smelling the new carpet,
Tests exams and homework will I ever forget.
Saying the word chocolate people think I'm mad,
Entering a hospital all of it makes me sad.
The sirens of a police car, I know something's wrong,
The sounds of howling winds, keeping me up all night long.
Touching frogs, spiders and ants they always make me shiver,
Having an empty stomach, leaving my vegetables and liver.
Going to the pub, smoke all in my face,
All I do is worry about cancer just in case.
Those were some of my worst things,
And that is what Emma Skelton brings.

Emma Skelton (12)
Millais School

An English Winter

Winter is coming and brings the cold,
With big long fires as in days of old.
As snowflakes tumble from the sky,
Wrapping presents a bow with tie.
The robin sits and sings his song
Father Christmas comes, we've waited so long.
Christmas dinner all around,
The atmosphere a lovely sound.
Opening presents, excited faces,
New toys and boots with laces.
The holiday ends and winter too,
Spring is coming, the lambs are new.

Ashton Tansey (12)
Millais School

Favourite Things

The smell of cream soda makes me float
And I love it when I can wear my new coat.
My little nephew smiles and dances round,
Pop and rock, that's my sound.
I enjoy the dark, bush night as the animals call
And a full day shopping at the mall.
I like the sound of my dog racing up the stairs,
And my brother calling 'Amy cheers!'
My favourite pop star is Britney Spears,
A cuddle with my dog calms all my fears.
The feel of my bed is cosy and nice,
I like it too when I can skate on ice.
I like to cuddle the soft hair on my dog Abbie,
When I have a fizzy drink I am very happy.
I like it when I wake in the morning
And I can smell my breakfast warming.
The smell of a barbecue on a hot, sunny day,
Sharing this with my family is the best way to play!

Amy McDonogh (11)
Millais School

Fear

I wave the bus goodbye,
I nearly start to cry,
I put the key in the slot,
I double lock the door,
My feet dragged on the floor,
I reach out for the phone,
Sitting all alone,
My hand slips on the phone,
I wish I wasn't alone.

Sinead Nugent (12)
Millais School

Bullying

I am being bullied,
I feel so alone,
They take me aside every day,
Oh please let me go home.

Pushing me in puddles,
Then running away,
Leaving me there, dirty and wet,
While they go off and play.

Can't tell Mum,
And can't tell Dad,
Can't tell anyone,
How they're making me sad.

Taking my lunch money,
Locking me out,
I just feel like hiding,
When they are about.

Watching the clock,
Is it time to go home?
Another day of sadness gone,
But I still feel all alone.

Charlotte Clark (11)
Millais School

Being Female

Girls don't fight,
In their diaries they prefer to write.
Body change occurs,
'Mine aren't as big as hers.'
Our make-up's our pride and joy,
Sometimes we really annoy (others).
We live long,
And forget what's right and wrong.
We love our hair
And really care.
When our babies are born,
We watch them till dawn.
We love wearing high heels
And keep to healthy meals.
When home-time arrives,
We don't bring out the knives.
We hate to say goodbye to our special friends,
Now the poem ends.

Allana Cheema (13)
Millais School

Tramp

I live on a cold, lonely street
With leaves running across the floor
At night people with homes walk past me
I feel left out and lonely people leave me
Sitting there all on my own
I would like a home that is my wish
I want a family who love and care about me
Like you I want to be loved by you!

Clare Munns (12)
Millais School

Myself

I see my reflection in the mirror.
I look pretty to me.
With my big chunky boots and baggy trousers
And my deep, dark make-up.

I walk outside.
Everybody stares and whispers.
'Look at her'
I'm not Miss Popular and I'm not Miss Loser.
I'm just right in the middle I guess.
As I cry myself up the street and into the fridge.
I grab the comfort food and crawl into bed
And say, 'Thank God I'm not one of them!'

As I listen to my music, full blast and loud.
I hear the neighbours screaming,
'Turn it down!'

Stop, look and listen all you losers.
I'm a girl who can cope in a modern day world
And all I have to say is,
'Thank God I'm not one of them!'

Stevie Rintoul (12)
Millais School

Amelia

A lonely girl is sitting alone,
M inding her own business,
E mptying her mind, like a moneybank,
L ooking for an ending to the lost story,
I magining forest, treasures and adventures,
A s a dragon flies by.

Amelia Bagwell (11)
Millais School

I Don't Want To Go To Nan's

I don't want to go to Nan's,
It smells all funny there.
A quite strong smell of lavender,
Is floating in the air.
I don't want to go to Nan's,
She gives me funny meals,
She makes me eat green vegetables,
But I'd rather pay her bills!
I don't want to go to Nan's,
I want to watch the telly,
I want to play in the street,
With chips in my belly!
I don't want to go to Nan's,
But Mum says that I have to,
So here I am at my Nan's,
Doing things I have to.

Georgina Trinder (12)
Millais School

Best Things

I love my bed as I curl up and drift away.
My teddy in my arms and here it will stay.
The sight of my little sister in her bed.
The crunchy smell of crispy bread.
The sweet smell of fresh strawberries and cream.
While watching EastEnders on the screen.
The sound of the sea in Cornwall bashing against the rocks.
As I sit in my armchair with long pink socks.
I love Tommy Girl perfume as I spray it on me
As I stand by the old oak tree.
The taste of a Big Mac and chips with lots of salt.
As I turn at the train station and see lots of nuts and bolts.
These are all my favourite things.

Charlotte Croucher (11)
Millais School

Hannah's Favourite Things

My mum's perfume fills the air,
The smell of scent from the garden chair.

Petrol shivers up my nose,
My sister sprays me with the hose.

Vanilla ice cream is so nice,
A cooked breakfast is much better than mice.
Christina Aguilera is the best,
Birds singing while I rest.

The rain falls hard upon the roof,
The tingle of ice cream on my tooth.

The touch of fluffy mats,
Is not as good as stroking a cat.

Up in the mountains high,
My personal stereo and hi-fi.

Hannah Gear (11)
Millais School

My Favourite Things

Watching the telly
With food in my belly.
Horses, dogs and cats,
But definitely not the rats.
Sliding and rolling down the hill,
Wishing I lived in a water mill
Blue birds and grey birds start to fly,
But unfortunately flowers die.
Christmas and birthdays could be the best,
But all Mum seems to do is rest!
Rosettes and certificates
Sitting on the wall,
Friends, family, but most of all
The best thing is . . . me!

Olivia Ince (11)
Millais School

Fear

I hear a dog in the distance.
I see a dog in the distance.

My heart starts thumping.
My blood starts pumping.

I feel sweat on my head.
I want the safety of my bed.

The dog comes near.
I cry out in fear.

The owner let's go.
I shout out no.

My leg starts shaking
My nerve starts breaking.

My body goes cold.
I wish I was bold.

I shout out and scream
I wish this was a dream!

Sonal Redkar (13)
Millais School

Best Foods!

All different puddings - I don't know why,
All sorts of crumbles and blackberry pie,
Jelly and custard, strawberries and cream,
Profiteroles are always a dream,
Ice cream sundaes, cheesecake too,
Fruits are very good for you,
Savoury dishes are also nice,
Chicken kebabs are great with rice,
I love roast dinners especially the meat,
Pasta dishes are always a treat,
I love all foods as you can see,
They all taste very nice to me!

Emily Edgington (11)
Millais School

My Favourite Things

I have a lot of favourite things,
But nothing like diamonds and gold ruby rings.
I like The Simpsons, Friends and Buffy the Vampire Slayer,
And watching good films on my DVD player.
Horror movies that make you jump out your skin,
Listening to bands and pop stars sing.
Dancing along to catchy tunes,
Swimming and going down water flumes.
Playing tennis in the park,
And watching fireworks light up the dark.
Going on holidays to have lots of fun,
Relaxing and sunbathing in the sun.
Drinking hot chocolate on cold winter nights,
Going to London and seeing the sights.
Reading books with lots of suspense,
And I hope to you this poem has made sense.
So now you see, I have a lot of favourite things,
But there is nothing like diamonds and gold ruby rings.

Jessica Fleig (11)
Millais School

Creature Of The Sea

Their rubbery skin is soft to feel,
Their fins are big and strong.
They love to eat fish as a meal,
In schools they swim along.
To chat they make a clicking sound,
Swim powerfully in the sea.
Plastic bags float around,
The dolphin's found his tea.
It thinks it's full, can eat no more,
The dolphin starves to death.
The beautiful creature I adore,
Has taken its very last breath.

Chloe Watson (12)
Millais School

The Sea

It laps against the shore,
With its big blue waves,
Swishing and swirling,
Inside secret caves.

For miles and miles,
Its waves carry on,
Tipping up boats
And singing its song.

It whistles and roars,
Glittering bright,
This big open space,
Twinkles in the night.

As the sun sets,
The sea shines red,
It's flowing and calm,
As the fish go to bed.

Emma Harmer (12)
Millais School

The Green-Eyed Monster

J ust like ivy, creeping up a wall.
E nvious, intolerant, green or grudging,
A ll are words with hatred feeling.
L ike a disease, so easy to catch,
O ut there to get you unless you fight back.
U ntying friendships, unwinding love.
S ilently entering the mind and all thoughts.
L ies are made to cover it up,
Y et it's still there hiding inside.

Emma Blagden (12)
Millais School

The Dead Of Night

Run, run, it's coming, it's crushing,
Run, run, it's gliding, it's sweeping,
Run, run, it's looking to get you,
The darkness is sprinting, taking control.

It's as dark as can be,
Jet black if you can see,
It's a piercing shadow,
Licking up your window.

Crouching beside your desk,
Scaring you at its best,
Shall I let out a scream,
Or just drift off and dream.

Hiding under my sheet
But wait, was that a creak,
Peeping out the top,
Waiting for it to drop.

Run, run, it's coming, it's crushing,
Run, run, it's gliding, it's sweeping,
Run, run, it's looking to get you,
The darkness is sprinting, taking control.

It's blinding, it's torture,
It's as hot as the core,
The sharpness of the light
Blinding at all its might.

The morning is here,
What a painstaking fear.

Lydia Playfoot (12)
Millais School

Mother

A lake,
A clear, unsullied sheet of glass.
Perfect and untouched.
Cradled in the arms of the mountains.
A mother protecting her child.
Her walls tower over the valley.
A harboured blanket of peace and humanity,
Over the wilderness where clouds sleep.

Night sweeps over.
Dark menacing clouds form.
Thunder rips through angry skies.
Lightning dances down to quivering meadows.
Rain savagely drums on disturbed waters.
Jet-black clouds disguise the moon's warm glow,
As shadows scurry to safety.

As a fresh new sun is born,
The curtain of mist is drawn away
By the mother's calm, comforting hands.
She watches intently over the joy in her arms.
The restored peace floats across the valley.
A clean slate after fury.
Cotton wool clouds sigh blissfully.
A land enveloped in incessant defence,
Just as a mother has everlasting love for her child.

Rebecca Attfield (14)
Millais School

A Season Poem

Spring is a beam of heat,
Spring is a field of yellow daffodils,
Spring is a waking alarm,
Spring is a year gone by
Taking us a leap ahead.

Summer is a flock of wheat,
Summer is a period for fox hound pups,
Summer is a desert extended for an open view,
Summer is a stick of glue for heat.

Autumn is a fall of leaves,
Autumn is a crispy crisp,
Autumn is a tree ready to have a new life,
Autumn is a bare rose ready to be covered
By a golden, green leaf scattered everywhere.

Winter is a pool of frosty ice,
Winter is a Christmas cracker,
Winter is a snowball waiting to be re-emerged
Winter is a bell ringing softly through the black air.

Lucinda Bryant (11)
Millais School

Dragon Fire

When the dragon blew his fire, it scorched the nearby land,
It reduced the town to cinders and left piles of sand,
The dragon thought that he had killed the nation's population,
In fact, when he blew his fire, it was time for celebration,
He pranced around, happy to have ruined many lives,
But little did he know, that the people did still survive,
For in winter, that country became extremely cold,
The people had a secret,
The fire just warmed their toes!

Tania Buckthorp (11)
Millais School

Seasons

Spring is a rose bud, waiting to bloom,
Spring is a dormouse, timid and shy,
Spring is a crystal clear stream,
Spring is a ball of new life and new joy.

Summer is the fire of a blazing hot sun,
Summer is a tiger, bold and bright,
Summer is a leaf, green until the end,
Summer is a volcano, exploding heat and growth.

Autumn is a golden and crimson lion's mane,
Autumn is a hurricane of swirling leaves,
Autumn is a blanket, made of many different colours,
Autumn is fire, beginning to die out.

Winter is an ice queen, frosty and cold,
Winter is a cake covered with icing sugar,
Winter is the end, until a new dawn,
Winter is the finale, in a show of seasonal life.

Alex Smith (11)
Millais School

Time

The moon will wax,
The moon will wane,
The tide will turn again and again.
The sands of time fall through and through,
Your life is slipping away from you.
Hands of a clock turn round and round,
The sun goes up, the sun sinks down.
The moon will rise,
The moon will fall,
This is time - it affects us all.

Rosie Hunt (13)
Millais School

Winter, Autumn, Spring, Summer

Winter is a white silk scarf
Winter is a wispy net curtain
Winter is a glistening curtain of diamonds
Winter is a shiny mirror of glass.

Autumn is a crunchy crisp packet
Autumn is a box of Maltesers
Autumn is a never-ending stream of tears
Autumn is a field of strawberries.

Spring is a cluster of blossom
Spring is silver, glittery glass
Spring is a newborn lamb
Spring is a beam of sunlight.

Summer is a juicy pineapple
Summer is a vase of shining sunflowers
Summer is hot, dripping butter
Summer is a golden desert that never ends.

Sarah Cheesman (11)
Millais School

Comets

Comets are like fiery angels
going to war with
the stars.

Comets are like fiery tears
coming from the
eyes of God.

Comets are like fiery raindrops
raining down
on Earth.

Comets are like rare, red diamonds
once seen
never forgotten.

Lauren Whittaker (12)
Millais School

A Night In Winter

Moonlight glows
As the sun goes
Stars come out to play
Twisting and turning along the way.

Fire fades
As darkness is made
The cold winds blow
And God will give us snow.

Snowflakes fall
Get out your shawl
Coldness is now completely spread
Find your heart and let it be led.

Animals creep
While children sleep
Minds go astray
Until the heart comes to stay.

Cats' eyes glare
When robins stare
Evergreens gleam
While flowers dream.

The sun awakes
Darkness escapes
Blankets of snow
Start to go.

Moonlight glows
As the sun goes
Stars come out to play
Twisting and turning along the way.

Sarah Kirby (11)
Millais School

Seasons

Spring is a lamb leaping from cloud to cloud
Spring is turning on a bright, shining light
Spring is a flower bursting out of a crowd
Spring is colours so bright.

Summer is ice creams melting away
Summer is a fire-breathing dragon's breath
Summer is silky, sandy, golden bays
Summer is a hot red pepper grown on a plant from the earth.

Autumn is a bright flame dying down
Autumn is a brown box, bare
Autumn is leaves covering the grass so that it drowns
Autumn is the grass being hugged by a big, brown bear.

Winter is a blanket of snow keeping the grass warm
Winter is sledging down snow-covered hills
Winter is the sun being torn
Winter is animals being chased by the chills.

The seasons are individual and special in their own ways
The seasons are there to give you different types of days.

Esther Johns (11)
Millais School

Summer

S unshine blazing into my day
C ausing burning on skin
O ut of this world, a million miles away
R ising over the hills to wake the world again
C atching eyes and always twinkling
H undreds of people lying in the sun
I mmense heat flaring through the clouds
N othing to make it die out
G oing down at last for the gloomy night.

Lois Johns (12)
Millais School

The Seasons

Spring is a baby chick cheeping into life.
Spring is the wind all around the world.
Spring is a leaf all fresh and bright.
Spring is the birds singing to the sun.

Summer is the heat on your face.
Summer is a roaring fire simmering and bright.
Summer is a flower dead and dry.
Summer is the grass all brown and gasping for liquid.

Autumn is the dreary leaves on the garden path.
Autumn is a rabbit alive but can change quickly.
Autumn is the wood on a chair all hard and brittle.
Autumn is the colour of fire from a baby dragon.

Winter is the sky all dark and cold.
Winter is the crisp ice on the windowpane.
Winter is the Christmas tree all pretty and lit up.
Winter is a dying fire all damp and dead.

Alice Emson (11)
Millais School

Ghost Ship

Waves crashed against the rocks,
As the boats docked.
The wind ran through my hair,
But did I dare
To take my boat out?
However I did not doubt,
That I was the only one out there.
Ghost ship, ghost ship.
I was a mile out to sea,
Then I saw the
Ghost ship, ghost ship.
But it ran into my boat
And it was to be,
The end of me.

Hannah Merryweather (11)
Millais School

Times!

Time, time, there's a time for everything:
A time for bath, a time for bed,
A time to eat and for books to read.
A time to have a break, a time to drink tea.
There's a time to be quiet and to simply be me.

Time, time, there's a time for everything:
A time to talk, a time for remembering,
A time to be happy, a time for crying.
A time to run, a time to walk,
A time to be silent and a time to talk.

Time, time, is there a time for everything?
There's a time for remembrance: the dead war heroes,
But what about the wounded, shaken from head to toe?
There's a time for making war, but what about peace?
It's a better use of time, so give peace a new lease.

Grace Carr (14)
Millais School

Making The World Happy

My favourite things
Are fancy rings,
Funny clowns
And yummy hash browns.
This is what makes the world happy.

My favourite thing
Is when a pop star sings,
Chocolate Hobnobs
And classy singing jobs.
This is what makes the world happy.

My favourite things
Are emotional feelings,
Pray to God,
This is what makes the world happy.

Pialada Preou (11)
Millais School

My Hamster Puzzle

M y hamster puzzle.
Y ou know how hamsters are.

H amsters are funny animals.
A nimals so small and furry.
M usic scares them if it's too loud.
S leeping is their daytime job.
T ired they often seem.
E ating is a hobby to them.
R aisins and nuts are best.

P uzzled they can be.
U p and down the stairs they climb.
Z ipping round all night in their nice big wheels.
Z igzagging around the furniture.
L ittle tender legs go very fast.
E njoy every minute of the night!

Hannah Stalley (12)
Millais School

Squirrels

I love squirrels, they climb like monkeys,
Soaring in the jungle.
They jump from tree to tree,
As smooth as a snake,
Their tails are bushy like
A porcupine's body.

I love squirrels even though
I've never touched them,
They would never hurt a single fly.

They run as quick as a cheetah
And are as mechanical as a machine
And they eat while staring as
Straight as an eagle.

Lily Gathercole (12)
Millais School

My Cat

My cat's called Dudley,
She's small and cuddly.
She is a tabby,
She's a little bit flabby.

My cat's coat is very thick,
Sometimes I take the mick.
She has sharp claws
And soft, padded paws.

My cat has lots of toys,
She is a girl, but we thought she was a boy.
She can be mean,
Sometimes she's never seen.

My cat sits in the bath
And everyone has a good laugh.
She plays in the rain,
She's such a pain.

Abigail Puttock (12)
Millais School

Death

You don't know what you've got till it's gone,
You never know when it's your turn,
You can never be too careful.
But never sit and worry because you can never predict it.
Most people have lots of questions, but I have only one . . .
What will Death look like?
People say Death will dress in black robes with a scythe in his hand.
But how do they know?
They don't know if Death's male or female,
Or if Death's black or white,
Or if Death's just a swirl of mist hovering above us waiting to strike.

Rhiannon Spencer (12)
Millais School

Little

I want to be little again,
    So I can crawl around on the ground,
    Like a tiger *roar!*
    So I can jump and spring
    And do nearly anything.
    So I can weep and cry
    And wish to fly.

I want to be little again,
    So I can shout and scream
    And lick all the bowls with custard and cream.
    So I can raise a hand and make a band,
    From all of Mum's old saucepans,
    So I can write and draw all over my dad's study door.

I want to be little again,
    So I don't have to do the chores
    And tidy my drawers.
    So I don't have to lay the table,
    I can forget about reading my fables.
    Make me brush my teeth, that's mean,
    Washing - I don't care if it keeps me clean.

Laura Gale (11)
Millais School

How?

How can it be
that we can't see
how time flies by
you and I?

How time
keeps passing through the mind
of every one of human kind?

How can we
not take time
to watch as we pass
the greenness of
the morning grass
and how
the daylight bright
turns into
that sparkling starry night?

So remember!
Take care
to give yourself that time
to stand and stare.

Alexandra Vacca (13)
Millais School

My Best Things

A freshly baked cake just ready to eat,
Settling down on a soft, comfy seat,
My mum, when she's not being mean,
I especially like Avril Lavigne,
I like going shopping (me and my friends),
Sometimes they drive me round the bend,
The taste of chocolate left in my mouth,
Going on holidays in the south,
Mmmm, ice cream and jelly,
Practically everything I see on telly,
I sure like jeans, oh and shoes
And staying round at my auntie Sue's,
My grandma's cooking and my dad,
Sometimes he goes totally mad,
Purple flowers and pink too,
It's a shame cos they'll all die soon,
Waking up on Christmas morning,
Reading books, when thoughts are dawning,
I could go on forever, but I'd never stop,
So it's time to go now, before I pop!

Kimberley Norris (11)
Millais School

My Grandma

My grandma's dead,
I think of her in my head.

My mum is upset,
But she always forgets
That my grandma is dead.

I sit on my bed,
Thinking of her
As she runs through my head.

Of good things, not bad,
At times I made her mad.
I never stop thinking of my grandma.

We went to the beach, the park,
Everywhere together,
And now she's gone I can't do anything.
I will think of her in my heart forever.

I wish and I wish
That my grandma was here with me,
But inside she is really -
Isn't she?

Holly Hill (12)
Millais School

The Storm Sets In

The storm arrived with a crash and a snarl,
Lightning slashed across the blackened sky,
Cutting the night into pieces,
Like a sharp, white knife.

The thunder rumbled furiously,
Terrifying the creatures all around,
Shaking up the land,
Like food in a blender.

The wind whipped the plants,
Buffeted the boughs of trees,
They creaked in agony
Before breaking and falling with a cry.

Birds screamed and cawed
To their friends,
As their homes fell under
The rule of the raging storm.

One last rumble of thunder,
One last splitting flash of lightning,
Before suddenly, to the world's relief,
The storm goes on its way.

Charlotte Draper (11)
Millais School

We Are Gone But Not Forgotten

We are gone but not forgotten,
We are dead but still alive,
We shall never see the dawn of another day,
Or live to see another bird being born.

We died for our country,
All of us alike,
In our one plea,
To set Great Britain free.

We achieved our goal,
But never returned,
We died on the way to our hero's welcome,
But at least we can say we set Great Britain free.

We are gone but never forgotten,
We are dead but still alive in your hearts,
We shall never see the dawn of another day,
Or live to see another bird born.

Shana Cox (11)
Millais School

Bullied

She looks into the distance and sees
Black.
The darkness swirls; a thick, hazy mist
Around her fragile body, devouring.
It pinches all over, an excruciating pain,
Warm tears leak from her swollen eyes.
The further she walks,
The more it burns.
Then she turns
And starts striding back.
A new power brews inside;
She will face them.

Holly Batchelor (12)
Millais School

My Likes And Dislikes

I like chocolate and sweets,
But not smelly feet.
I like doughnuts,
But not nasty cuts.

I like Tammy and New Look,
But not to cook.
I like iced buns,
But not the sun.

I like German and French,
But not to sit on the bench.
I like little pups,
But not make-up.

I like books and London Bridge,
But not the fridge.
I like to work the cogs,
But not to cut the log.

I like sugar and candy,
But not the Dandy.
I like many things,
But not kings!

Rebecca Owen (12)
Millais School

The London Underground

We're going deeper, deeper, deeper
Underground
Can you feel the artificial cool?
We're going deeper, deeper, deeper
Underground
Can you hear the roar?
We're going deeper, deeper, deeper
Underground
Can you taste the stale air?
We're going deeper, deeper, deeper
Underground
Can you smell the polluted air?
We're going deeper, deeper, deeper
Underground
Can you see the tunnel?
We're going deeper, deeper, deeper
Underground
Can you see the rushing train?

Paulina Morvik (11)
Millais School

Lost

Unknown voices scattering around
The path is nowhere to be found
Upset, drowning in a river of tears
I really don't want to confront my fears

Where are all the friendly faces
We are torn apart in different places
Do they know I'm really lost
Or when I'm found will they be cross?

Why won't this nightmare ever end
I can't think, it's driving me around the bend
Running, running away from my worries
I need to get back, I need to hurry
I'm lost.

Rebecca Nash (12)
Millais School

I Will Put In My Box . . .

(Based on 'Magic Box' by Kit Wright)

I will put in my box . . .
The sweet smell of a tiny baby,
Its first cry,
I will put in my box . . .
The hot fire of a dragon,
As hot as an oven.
I will put in my box . . .
The sour taste of my favourite sweet,
Fizzing in my mouth.
I will put in my box . . .
The musty smell of the PE cupboard,
From sweaty football shirts.
I will put in my box . . .
A piece of straw from an old man's hut years ago.
I will put in my box . . .
The fishes from the ocean,
A shark's tooth.
My box is made from the finest silks in the world,
The riches of my grandad.
It has rings of my first hair.
I like my box because it keeps all my things safe.

Emily Miles (11)
Millais School

Unknown/Gone

I sat there, waiting for it to come.
Hours passed, there was still no sign.
It wasn't coming, I knew it wouldn't.
I got up, ready to go.
But then, it came like a cheetah,
Running in a field.
I got in, I needed to get there fast.
We moved swiftly, but silently,
They were standing, watching us.
I looked out of the window,
Watching as we went by.
We stopped, they told me to get out.
This wasn't where I was going.
They put me in line,
Then it happened - *rat-a-tata, tata, tata, tata, tata.*
Gone!

Emily Chetty (12)
Millais School

Out Of Control

First it was the crackle of an open fire,
Then the people started to tire.
The small fire got bigger and bigger
And blazed out of control.
The screams, the cries as the fire roared,
The terrified eyes as the fire died when the rain started to fall.

The roof started to tumble down,
The little child's face creased from the sound.
The rain was lashing on the people's faces,
The people thankful as the fire subsided.
Then suddenly, as if out of nowhere,
A beautiful rainbow appeared.

Aimée Leverett (12)
Millais School

Please Let This Season Never End

Quick, let's go, let's get on the plane.
Flying over ocean and land,
Waiting for the destination to come into view.
Finally we are there, after all those hours.
Caribbean sun beating down on our heads,
Soaking up the sun for a great tan.
Please let this season never end.

Plants bob up above the soil,
They spread their petals and produce new life,
Colourful and scented, as beautiful as can be.
Newborn lambs, soft and cuddly,
Bleating in the fields,
Waiting for their mothers to come and join them.
Please let this season never end.

Colours start to change on the leaves of the trees,
Oranges, reds and yellows.
As time goes by, the leaves drop to the forest floor.
Nights draw in, the world becomes black.
The moon comes out, it casts shadows on the Earth.
The world goes silent, everybody sleeps.
Please let this season never end.

Children play on the crisp snow,
Chucking snowballs and sledging.
Smiles upon everyone's faces.
Christmas lights shine so bright,
Gifts and presents stacked under the tree,
Mistletoe hangs off the ceiling.
Please let this season never end.

Victoria Gardiner (13)
Millais School

Wolf

His beady, golden eyes,
His smoky-grey coat,
His eyes full of wisdom
And his coat tattered with blood.

He pads through the snow,
Silent,
With only tracks to show
Where this creature walked.

He stalks his prey,
Eagerness in his eyes,
He runs like a bullet,
A scream high-pitched, a note of death.

Bright-red blood,
Staining the pure white snow,
He walks on,
His belly full.

Amy Dimmock (12)
Millais School

In The Library

All is silent in the library,
Then suddenly shadows leap from shelf to shelf,
Candles appear, flickering brightly
And out come the characters from the books.

Peter Pan and Captain Hook
And many a more devious crook.
Fairy godmothers and wicked witches,
Harry Potter and golden Snitches.

They dance around the floor at midnight,
Until the dawn breaks.
At last returning back to their books,
So you can read all about them.

Joanne Marychurch (13)
Millais School

Winter Nights

Fire crackling with an orange glow,
Children staring out at the wondrous snow.
Marshmallows around a campfire at night,
Streets lit up by the glistening moonlight.

Cats are all snuggly in their cosy, warm beds,
Tails under their tummies, paws by their head.
Families are playing their favourite board game,
Cluedo, Monopoly, charades - what's the name?

New Year is now nearing,
Fireworks and cheering.
Cute celebration collars on kittens,
People are wearing woolly hats and mittens.

Doorbells are rung,
Carols are sung.
Many hearts are warmed,
Many friendships are formed.

Emma Wilson (12)
Millais School

Bush Fire

They were silent
The wind made its way through the soldiers standing tall.
They were chatting
They swished and swayed like a horse's tail.

They smiled
The rolling wind sped past, punching his fists.
They danced
The sun crept slowly in.

They screamed
Suddenly a blaze of light
There blackened
A blanket of ash floor.

Jade Azhar (12)
Millais School

Earthquakes

The rumble was shaking the Earth apart
like the tearing of paper.
The black hole was closing in
like the night sky holding back the light.

Suddenly the floor started to crack.
The tremble of the earth, the crushing of houses and trees
like splitting up a family.

The faint whispers of the children's cries.
The look of fear in their eyes.
The tears roll down as the emotion
creeps down the everlasting roads of holes dug deep.

The rescue workers search all day, finding bodies along their way.
Digging down underground,
listening hard for any sound.

Rebecca Armstrong (12)
Millais School

The Devil's Beast

Crackling gently against the silent night,
An orange glow in the moonlit sky,
Harmless sparks fly to darkness,
Splintering twigs wake the sleeping world,
Flickering like a serpent's tongue.

The wind picks up, the fire grows,
Flames lash out to overhanging branches.
The cracking and splintering are ten times louder,
Orange and red flames rise to the moon.
Let this fire burn brighter tonight.

Roaring in the mystic darkness,
Climbing up like a devil's beast.
A rush of water, a twister of smoke,
In a click of a finger, this raging fire has gone out.
Nothing is left in this deserted world.

Alison Campbell (12)
Millais School

The Free One

The air, it wrestles against
the manumission of the undomesticated
individual.

It is in its own psychological world,
it cannot heed a word of sympathy,
nor converse the word of sense.

The unmitigated flow of its silken mane,
it suggests lonesomeness unbreakable, and
ignorance.
Yet the twinkling shimmer in its unfathomable eye,
it gives a soft, soothing scent to its alluring movement.

Its black, resplendent coat glistens like the moonlight,
its elegance brings a bitter fragment to my bone.
Many people go up to it,
yet its awesome power, it coerces them away.

It appears so Herculean and robust,
its destructive hooves demolish the ground.
Ostentatiously it gallops along,
in its heart only liberty can be inaugurated.

Lorna-Belle Harty (12)
Millais School

Destruction

Death, destruction and disaster,
Just because of a volcano's anger,
Danger, don't go near,
Scorching-hot lava.
Trampling through the undergrowth,
Stunning everything forever,
That's in its path.
The ash and smoke,
Blinding and choking,
Changing the land forever.
People run from their homes,
Birds and animals flee,
Taking their young with them,
To the safe countryside miles away.
Will they make it?
When all is calm, they return to their homes,
Always afraid that their bad-tempered neighbour
Would explode again.

Megan Clark (12)
Millais School

Untitled

Mystery in the air,
Greyness, all around,
Everywhere I turn.
The stillness, stillness, stillness.
The silence, so silent, so deadly.
What will happen next?

The wind whistles through my hair,
Stormclouds gather overhead.
The darkness swirls in.

A drop of water,
More, more!

Slow at first,
A cold, dripping tap,
Getting faster, colder,
So, so vicious.

Next, the hail,
Splashing!
Crashing!
Smashing!
Splintering the calm water.
When will it stop?

Like buckets of stones,
The hail slaps down,
Like a large hand hitting the sea.

Wild! Windy!
Large drops of water
From waves as huge as a building.

Slowly, the rage of the rain
Stops, and the night is calm
Again.

Lucy Elkins (12)
Millais School

Fireworks

It's dark and quiet, the dead of night,
Then suddenly comes a flash of light.
Colours exploding in the sky,
The sparkles reflected in every eye.

Little kids run inside,
From the crashes and bangs they need to hide.
Excitement and tension in the air,
Moving like dancers without any care.

Clatters and whooshes spill out to the stars,
People stop in the road and look out from their cars.
Sparklers held in gloved hands burn strong,
Spitting and hissing and singing their song.

Colours and noise put together as one,
One minute it's silence, then a bang like a gun.
Emotions are racing, excitement and fear,
But you only get fireworks once every year.

Martha Allsop (13)
Millais School

The Fire Friend

Crackle, the flames are high in the air,
the flames are like a lion - dangerous but beautiful,
the colours glow in the dead of the night,
I see red, yellow, orange and gold,
a story of mystery for you to unfold.

Roar, the fire it grows louder and louder,
the ash in your eyes making you squint,
but you can't resist throwing things in,
I hear crackling, roaring and soft, comforting whistles,
softer than cotton, sharper than thistles.

Slurp, I drink as I sit by the fire,
warming my lips and keeping me happy,
I feel so relaxed with the fire burning,
I feel cosy, warm, secure, not alone,
the fire's a friend, warming my home.

April Loft (12)
Millais School

The Holiday Fire

Sitting in a misty car
In front, a fierce fire framing
The black silhouette of a burned out car.

Car crash
One minute driving,
Next minute tumbling . . .
Tumbling over and over.
Later we heard the news -
A two week old baby and
A thirty-one year old man died.

Ryan Hunter (11)
Rydon Community College

Time To Impress

Excitement mounting
Reddening faces
Performance started
Scene four was here

I practised hard and learned my lines
Name is called
Take a deep breath
It's now time to impress

I looked the part
In leather and chains
Frightening the parents
With, 'I'm a rat leader, OK?'

Starting to enjoy
Not as hard as I thought
Crowd clapping, wild applause
I leave the stage, proud as can be.

Congratulations all round
All I feel is relief
A glow of a job well done
Will I do it again? I think so.

Rachael Ann Lewis (11)
Rydon Community College

The Butterfly

I'm a butterfly
I have colourful wings
I flutter around all day
In the high winds

I'm a butterfly
Small and fast
When I have a race
I never come last.

Amy Gooding (11)
Rydon Community College

Theme Park

Today we were going
Going to a theme park
I was excited
Excited to go on the rides.

The scary rides were busy
Busy with people waiting
The cries and screams were loud
And they filled the air.

The log flume was slow
Slow apart from the slope
That went down
Down to the spraying water

Tidal was fast
Fast when it got to the top
And went *splash* into
The spraying water.

I hope to go again soon.

Amber Leask (12)
Rydon Community College

Monkeys

I am a monkey, I'm cuddly and fun
I am a monkey, I love the sun.
I am a monkey, I would like a bun,
I am a monkey, please could I have one?

I am a monkey swinging from a tree
I am a monkey, hey watch me!
I am a monkey I'm being chased by a bee,
I am a monkey, it stung me!

I am a monkey and I grumble,
I am a monkey and I stumbled.
I am a monkey, I like rough and tumble,
I am a monkey, I live in the jungle.

Enna O'Connor (10)
Rydon Community College

Disney Parade

My stomach jumped
I shook all over
And butterflies flew inside me.

My throat tickled
My eyes glared around me
And I realised I wasn't in a dream.

In Disneyland Paris
I was ready to dance
I did my final practise.

The music started
The huge gates opened
And the parade had just began.

I looked around, beaming like mad
Seeing eyes glaring back at me.
I scanned the crowds trying to find my mum.

I finally saw her
The butterflies escaped to far away
And suddenly the music stopped.

I was sad to see the end
So I took one last look at the crowd
And then I had to go.

Mixed feelings were inside me,
Swishing around from happy to sad.
The parade had finished just like that.

It's now just a memory
But as I think it through,
I feel like I'm there again.

Lauren Handley (11)
Rydon Community College

The Secret

Staring - staring like a cat caught in the light,
something - something in my head
was telling me it's not right.

Lord oh Lord, give me a sign. A sign of love
a sign of peace something to tell me
everything is fine.

But nothing was fine, I had taken something
that was not mine.

I closed my eyes and tried to sleep,
I tossed and turned my heart sank deep.

I know it's not right, I know it's all wrong,
something goes back to whom it belongs.

I know it's right
I know what's wrong,
something's going back to whom it belongs.

I know it's right
I know what's wrong
something's gone back to whom it belongs.

Bonnie Airlie (11)
Rydon Community College

The Angel's World

Excitedly the warm, musty cocoon beckoned
Me into the plane.
Forced into a confined space
Between seat and side,
Streamlined dust going out the door.

Nervously I sat down with the sun in my eyes,
My excited Mum plunged down into the seat,
Waiting worriedly for the ride of my life.

Excitedly engines whined with a deep, powerful throb,
Triumphantly the plane entered first at the runway,
Engine's mechanical heartbeat grew louder and louder,
Plane cranking higher and higher like a bird through the air.

We climbed through the heavens above,
Into what seemed like the angel's, mystical world.
There we lingered, exploring the forgotten world,
Time was up and we descended into our mundane cage.

Dan Pease (11)
Rydon Community College

Computer Oh Computer

C omputer, oh computer
O h will you help me?
M y work is a mess and I don't understand
P lease could you help me?
U nimaginable brain! Computer you're the cleverest in our house.
T ogether we can work it through
E venly, quick typing
R ead, spell check and print.

Emily Moss (10)
Rydon Community College

Football Poem

I felt nervous
Butterflies were in my stomach
Adrenaline rushing through my body
I shivered.

The whistle due to go
I hold my breath in expectation,
Will we win or will we come to woe
In the meantime, I stumble, racing into position.

Two-nil down
Frustrated and annoyed
Missing all the chances
We were approaching full-time.

Dangerous corner, swerving round
Bang! I headed and it's a goal.
I've scored on my debut
Yes! Yes! Yes!

Running back calmly,
Not celebrating mad.
Don't want to embarrass myself
They will think I'm sad.

Sweating profusely
I come off the pitch
Drat, we lost,
And I've got a stitch.

Tristan Mann (11)
Rydon Community College

My Poem

I went to bed
And I broke my head,
So I've sewn it with a piece of thread
And a slice of bread.
My door was red
So I went back to bed
And I broke my chin,
So I put it in the bin,
It's wonderful to be me,
I can see a bee
On my knee
I can see a giraffe,
In my bath.
This is my poem
And my mum says it's by Michael Owen.

William Lawson-Maycock (13)
Rydon Community College

Winter

Snowflakes softly come drifting down
Twisting round and round and round,
Children playing in the snow
Watching Santa saying, 'Ho! Ho! Ho!'

Standing warmly by the fire
Watching sparks fly
Warming up your small cold toes
As the stars go by.

Sitting on your beds
With your stockings hanging up
Waiting to hear a great big thump
And Santa drinking from his cup.

Tasmine Graffy (10)
Rydon Community College

Life

In the beginning life was so simple
So perfect was every dimple
We just played and danced
And we all had a second chance.

The years float by like clouds
All the year 5s in their crowds.
The books and writing, games and things
School starts and learning begins.

Primary seems to disappear
And soon we all begin to fear,
The year 8s in their secondary school
With it's gym, stage and huge blue pool.

Soon we'll be moving on again
And I have to say it will be a shame
But I know some day, I will remember
The changes that happen every September.

And I'll think maybe it was all worth it
All the responsibilities and pain will fit
And maybe I'll believe in *forever*
And maybe I'll understand *never!*

Or maybe I'll just contemplate *life!*

Abigail Lepine (12)
Rydon Community College

Last Flight

The eagle fluttered her wings
Raising her head to the warm wind
Morsels of rabbit forgotten
In the ultimate desire for flight
Last preen of silk, black feathers
No more nests to make
Flying silently out of the niche
Wind brushing her feathers
This would be her last flight
Her wings slicing through the air
Flying she loved
Slowly she glided down to a cliff
And lay down, spreading her wings
Lying still
A murmur of birds
Silence
Apart from a cool breeze
As she slept in peace -
Motionless.

Rachel Bell (12)
Rydon Community College

The Lady Of Shalott - Part V

(Based on 'The Lady Of Shalott' by Alfred Lord Tennyson)

As she passed, the ladies cried
Lancelot ran down to her side
Against the will of the river's tide.
The signal of the black cat tried
To bring him back to Camelot.
On the boat she lay
Sir Lancelot will forever stay,
The wind howled as the boat slowly sank away
The Lady of Shalott.

Katharine Childs (12)
Rydon Community College

Flight

Flight: It can be anything
A flight of stairs . . .
You walk up them, you walk down them.
Baby's cry on them, cats puke on them.
The disabled can't use them . . . well, they need a lift!
Kiddies fall over them and break their necks,
Well stairs can do many things.

A flight: plane.
You go up, your ears pop.
Flights are steep, high and you soar.
They can be smooth or bumpy and planes need speed,
Fighting for more and more.
Greedy, that's what they are!

A flight from reality: drugs,
Have some and you believe you can do anything.
Jump out of a plane and not get hurt!
Jump off the Eiffel Tower and fly like superman
Well . . . you fall to your death
And never come back to this Earth,
You go to the fires of Hell,
Tormented by the man you laughed about
The one and only Satan!
You would have to be a fool to take drugs.

And one more, the ultimate flight: death.
It can come unexpectedly, just walking across the road,
Someone speeding.
You have your life flashing by you, your last moments
Then . . . blackness.
Your life, wasted.

Lewis Crook (12)
Rydon Community College

Flight!

Flight is a liberating sensation
Looking down freely on the entire nation
The ability to fly is a wonderful thing
Going higher and higher than birds under wing

Flight will evoke feelings of peace
Ensuring our worries will surely soon cease
Whether by plane or whether by parachute
The surrounding sounds just seem too mute

You can feel with elation, the pure, clean air
That flows so gently through your hair
No limit is set to the height you can go
The distance to Heaven appears a stone's throw

Your position is elevated high above the clouds
In the still, dark night you can see bright stars crowd
There's no feeling like it and no greater sight
Than the vision, the sounds, the sensation of flight.

Matthew Carmichael (12)
Rydon Community College

The Alley Cat

Stalking through the trees
Running up the hill
Creeping in the bushes by the old, deserted mill.
Hiding in the alley
Sleeping behind a bin
Being treated badly, when it makes a din.
We have them in our homes
They are things we love and cherish
Just because they're not ours -
Why do we call them a menace?

Sam Grantham (11)
Rydon Community College

Rocket Launch

5, 4, 3, 2, 1 . . . ready to take-off!
With a surge of excitement, I lifted off the ground
Going up and up, leaving the world behind me
The stars beckoned, pulling me towards them
The pole star was shining way above me
I found myself looking this way and that
The view was so different from up here
The flight stopped abruptly, I came to my journey's end
It looked bleak and deserted, not homely at all
The first step I took felt more like a leap than a step
The moon felt cold and wet
No wind to warm me up, no gravity to keep me down
I wanted to stay although it was lonely
Well I've been to the moon and back
I've seen what it's like, bleak, deserted, cold and wet.

Lucie Kibblewhite (12)
Rydon Community College

My Poem

Tiptoeing in silence towards the edge
My heart is thumping
My legs are bumping
Looking down
It's a long, long way
Suddenly I start to topple.
Falling down, down, down
Flight is wonderful
Flight is scary
Gliding through the air.
With the wind racing through my hair
I see something blue shimmer near me
I have been dreading this moment
Nearer and nearer I get . . .
Splash!

Lucy Seymour (12)
Rydon Community College

Flight

It felt like hours to me,
but it was seconds in reality
the feeling was torture
once the uneasy detour was over.
All I could see was fuzzy and grey,
I thought I wouldn't see passed that day.
The drop was so steep,
I now wish I didn't leap.
Wind blowing through my hair
I didn't mind, I didn't care.
A vertical horizon, view,
not many knew what I would do.
My ears popped, forever high,
it felt like I was falling from a cloud in the sky.
My stomach tightened,
feeling so frightened,
tears sticking to my eyes,
head first, then my thighs.
I heard screaming from down below,
probably my mum, I'll never know.
I was numbly cold
I wasn't going to die of being old.
Good times rushed to my head,
Even the bad dreams I've had in bed.
I felt so light
like a child's kite,
Soaring through the wind,
levitating, as I unconsciously grinned.
Freedom was knocking at my door
but not for long, I wasn't far from the floor.
My life was hanging on a loose hook,
I didn't dare open my eyes to look.
The further down I flew
the conquest grew,
my fears have been overlooked,
Detonator, the power to be mistook.

Victoria Etheridge (12)
Rydon Community College

The Flight

Flying over Paradise
I glide over the silent waters
Hovering over the swaying, palm trees
I often stop and wonder
When I fly swiftly, like a bird
When I soar high above the Earth
When a sense of freedom hits me
When on the clouds, I surf
When calming music shivers down my spine
When the wind brushes past my ears
When floating in the sky
When drifting from my fears
I look back down at the white beaches
It's when I stop to stare
Is this truly Paradise!
Did I really care?
Escaping from my problems
That one day I had to face
It wasn't a solution
Hiding in this maze
I have to do things right now
Right is always best
But what is right and what is wrong?
Just have faith, let your heart do the rest.

Maxine Kwok (12)
Rydon Community College

My Poem

Trudging through a flooded forest of trees
I'm freezing, I'm shaking, especially my knees
It is only October, on my birthday
Why are we here? I hear you say
We are here to play paintball
We get to a camp, wooden and tall
They tell us to put on a suit and a mask
Ready to start our painty task
We collected our guns and he explained the rules
These rules are obvious, do they think we are fools?
When we started the game, I ran for cover
Ready to shoot my enemy, my brother
When I first saw them, I shot and shot
Bringing down two to lie and rot
We covered the other two in paint with ease
With four on my team, this was not a tight squeeze!

Joe Russell (11)
Rydon Community College

The Lady Of Shalott - Part V

(Based on 'The Lady Of Shalott' by Alfred Lord Tennyson)

And now still as of long ago,
The people wander to and fro,
But tell each other as they go.
For now the smallest child will know
This tale of Camelot;
For brother, sister, husband and wife,
Are doomed to live in eternal strife,
For she has torn the joy from life,
The Lady of Shalott.

Max Hardie (12)
Rydon Community College

Before It Happened

Shy and timid I was then, before it happened,
Never spoke, never said my point of view.
The operation on my ears was going to change it all.
I would be bold, I would be confident
I would get big parts in our play.
But what if it went wrong?
What if I didn't wake up?
Would it damage me for life?
No, my ears would be pinned back perfectly -
Wouldn't they?

Before I knew it, I was in a hospital bed,
Being injected to put me to sleep.
Doctors pushing and pulling at my ears,
Yet me, none the wiser!
When woken up, I was so tired and so hungry.

After the op, I was really happy,
I was bold, I was confident.
I got my parts in the play
I was a totally different person.
The shy, timid person had gone
And an unknown person had landed.
It did me so much good!

Johanna Stevens-Yule (11)
Rydon Community College

My Best Friend

Eyes sombre and doubtful, can it be true?
Won't believe, shan't let her leave
My other half, to be torn away
Plucked from me by her family
Tossed like a die
To the other side of the globe

Tears overwhelmed me, turmoil breaks free
The noxious serpent
With fangs to penetrate me
Contaminates and spreads loneliness
It wound its coils about my neck
Day by day it increases its grip

I shrouded myself inside a cocoon
Safe and unsensing
Built to feel no pain
That fateful day, that dreadful hour
Comes closer, closer to haunt me

The day that she left was the day my life ended
Into the shadows away from the light
My tears and the sun merged into one
Pressed close to the window
I have to forsake her
I could see her reflection long after she'd gone.

Ellen Friend (12)
Rydon Community College

My Favourite Day

Whiling away my time,
While the train ate up the miles,
To then reach journey's end.

Slowly trudging to the hotel,
Weighed down by the baggage.

Our spirits rapidly rising,
Energy boiling through,
Gasping to escape
But died down rapidly
Before the show.
Could not remember anything
Nerves too much.

Dancing in Disney, all went well
I danced and did my best.
The rides were great
They filled me with excitement.
That was my favourite day.

Jess Rolland (11)
Rydon Community College

The Lady Of Shalott - Part 5
(Based on 'The Lady Of Shalott' by Alfred Lord Tennyson)

Beneath a marble slab she was laid
In a grave, Sir Lancelot made.
Each day he came and wept and prayed
There she was and there she stayed,
Beside tower'd Camelot;
Her body gone, her soul is near
Each morning the knights swear they hear.
Her songs are heard, loud and clear
The Lady of Shalott.

Lee Baker (12)
Rydon Community College

Taking The 11+

The dreaded day had come
The terrible Monday was true,
It was one of those grey mornings
Happy feelings were few.

The preparation was tense
The atmosphere was mild,
Around the house was quiet
My butterflies went wild.

I arrived at school to worry
But everything was normal,
Running, screaming, shouting
Nobody was acting formal!

The room was cramped
It felt like all eyes were on me.
I was going to crack with fear
The test was all I could see.

The time limit was short
But the speed it went, was quicker,
For the first few minutes I panicked
I did not dare to move or flicker.

I made a mistake
I started to tremble and shake,
I erased it out quickly
My whole body began to quake.

In the end I finished in style
And came out with a smile,
The shivers were still in my seat
But the shakes had left my feet!

James Cooperwaite (11)
Rydon Community College

The Titan

The hot Texas air rushed into my face as I got out,
We were at Six Flags Theme Park, I stretched with a shout
We looked straight up and there it was,
The Titan in the hot sun.
Colby followed and when she saw
The first thing she said was,
'That's gotta be breaking the law!'
We queued and we thought it would never end,
It was totally driving my sister round the bend.
We were on The Titan, I was scared to death,
We were about to meet a vertical drop,
I really badly wanted this thing to stop.
'Oh my God! Oh my God! Oh my God!' I screamed
When I got off I was so surprised,
My face was a total disguise.
I looked really happy but I felt really bad
But I didn't feel the one bit sad.

Ed Mishan (11)
Rydon Community College

Another Chance
(In loving memory of my kitten, Toby)

If Death had given him another chance
He would still be in my arms
But that's the way it had to go
I will never feel his fur on my palms.

I loved him with all my heart,
I wish he was still here.
But that's the way it had to go
I'm giving him another tear.

He is there and I am here
I wish he was with me
But that's the way it had to be
I loved my cat Toby.

Eleanor Brough (11)
Rydon Community College

Our Trip To Colorado

We were in Breckenridge
Lots of sausages in the fridge
I was with Torrence playing pool
He kept saying, 'It's pretty cool!'

You lot, staying here with us
My mum and dad made so much fuss
About how we were going to behave
Dad's almost forgotten to shave

We made a small snow cave
in the woods
Packed it with sweets
and loads of goods
Ice fishing, cold but dazzling bright
The fish came out but put up a fight
Snowmobile tracks through the snow
with their drone
Now see the warm lights of
welcoming home.

Matt Goring (11)
Rydon Community College

Grey Heron

We walked through the wet grasslands and there
We saw it flying high in the sky.
His wings soaring quietly.
The silent bird lands at the river's edge.
It wades in . . .
He steals an unfortunate fish from the gentle water.
Out of nowhere his companion swoops down beside him,
Together they fly and land on a leafless tree.
The sun is starting to set and the two silhouettes
Of the elegant birds soar peacefully in the air.
It's a heron, a grey heron.

Sadie J Craigie (10)
Rydon Community College

The Time Has Come!

Tarmac, strange underfoot
Pins and needles racking my leg,
I hobbled to the park gate
Excitement running through my head.

Slowly I walked into a world of fun and craze,
People eating,
People laughing.
Everywhere I went, people were joyful and happy.

Then I saw it, *Oblivion* in big letters,
I opened my mouth in excitement,
I was gobsmacked!
I sprinted to the entrance.

Fast and furious I went
It was strong and high,
Taking us on that journey
As it reached up to the sky.

All too soon it was over, and
I got on the coach.
We drove away, remembering,
Waiting for another day.

Jamie Claydon (11)
Rydon Community College

Silver Nods

Nodding away
On the Seychelles Island,
Perching on rocks
Showing off their rhythmic boogie.

Their button eyes gleaming in the sun,
As they glide silently
To the place where they belong
And their silver feathers bow to the king,
They will not be in danger on the king's command.

Greeting everyone who passes in search of food,
They find delicious mango scraps and fish,
Yellow stains trickling down their soft feathers,
When the Nodders are full, they take flight again
And circle round the tropical island in safety.

Weaving in and out of trees and hovering over plants,
Spying on a mate,
A lonely Nodder is ready to be a father,
He stretched out his enormous wings
Waiting for his wife to come.

As night falls
And the sun dies into the ocean floor.
The Nodders nod off to sleep
Until the sun rises once more.

Georgina Briggs (10)
Rydon Community College

The Golden Eagle

Golden eagles in the sky
Soaring higher as they fly.

Fluffy feathers, brown and bright,
Glistening in the warm sunlight.

A bundle of sticks for a nest
Repaired each year to look its best.

Circling in the sky each day,
Then thrust toward their innocent prey.

Majestic birds who rule the sky
Zooming through clouds as they fly.

They swoop and dive and search the mountains,
Hunting for food on their daily outings.

George Carter (10)
Rydon Community College

Not A Good Day

I wake up in the morning
And it's raining outside.
'Mum, where's my school bag?'
'Look for it!' she replies.

I pack my bag
For the tiring school day.
My mum shouted, 'Your homework!'
As I was walking away.

As I walked into school
It occurred to me
That I was missing something important
Which the teacher needs to see!

It was only my maths homework
Which I had left behind.
My mum had brought it up to school
How kind!

George Lindsay (13)
The Angmering School

Watch Out

Watch out! Watch out!
Whoever you are!
Quickly, quickly!
Into your car!
The Reaper's here!
He comes to kill
To rip, to slay
He comes to
Make us pay.

Into your car
Out of the streets.
Quickly, quickly!
He'll kill whom he meets.
The reaper's here!
He comes to hurt,
To scare, to taunt.
He comes to tear
Until the dawn.

John Ash (11)
The Angmering School

Will I Make It?

As I kick off, my wheels spin round
My heart takes a leap as my feet leave the ground
As I look down, the floor comes up close
Then my board hits the floor, I roll away, time to boast.

I shuffle my feet, putting them into place
I'm going so fast the wind whips at my face
As the gap looms up ahead, I turn my truck
The gap's cleared with ease, who needs good luck?

The first two gaps weren't that hard, I look for a third
The gap in front is so big, I'll need to soar like a bird
I come close to the edge, will I make it this time
I trip and I bail, please call 999!

Ben Marshall (13)
The Angmering School

Disaster Day

Disaster day
I do not like
the luck you bring
the sadness, the anger
that makes you
hate everything.

Disaster day
I do not like
the loneliness you share
the separation, the unhappiness
that makes you
think nobody cares.

Disaster day
I do not like
the frustration you make
the gloominess, the emptiness
that makes you
feel trapped.

Amy Haddon (11)
The Angmering School

Terrorist Attack

People crying, the damage is done
The bomb had already exploded
The terrorist had won
People fleeing from the screen of attack
Lives have gone and they will never come back.

People killed, everyone's upset
There's nothing they can do.
So many lives have been wrecked
Medics roll in to help the needy ones.

Hattie Jenkins (13)
The Angmering School

I Saw Him There Yesterday

Sleeping in the rain
What shall I do?
He must be in a lot of pain
I saw him there yesterday,
Rats sleeping in his bed.
Flies hovering over his head,
I saw him there yesterday
Cars driving by.
I can't help him, except cry!
I saw him there yesterday
Still as a rock,
Sleeping near the dock.
I saw him there yesterday,
Sleeping in the damp.
But he's nothing but a tramp.

Craig Ball (13)
The Angmering School

The Dodo Birds

Dodo birds were funny things
With long tails and feathered wings,
They walked round and round all day
And up and down in every way.
But once upon a summer's night
The Dodo birds were out of sight.

Some old people reported a bang!
Meanwhile others said a clang!
Hunters had been out that night
They had given the birds a fright.
The police were on the case
They set off a round the world chase.

Then the police stopped to think
The Dodo birds must be extinct!

Stacey Pellett (12)
The Angmering School

Rugby

Pointy Posts
I went to a rugby match and saw a -
Bouncy ball being kicked by the
Faulty fly-half being tackled by the
Forgetful flanker who passes to the
Crushing centre runs past the
Hunky hooker who trips over the
Lanky linesman, who flags up the
Wicked winger for swearing at the
Sexy scum-half who moans at the
Rough referee who blows up the
Flying fullback for passing forward, so the
Proud props lock in for a scrum then the
Stubborn second row lock in and they get the ball out to the
Bulky backs who get past the
Fierce forwards and they
Score! The conversion has been kicked over the
Pointy posts and it is!

Jack Metters (12)
The Angmering School

My Poem

I think of you and your eyes so blue
I feel so happy you make me go dappy
I blow on you and my wish came true
My wish that I could be with you

But somehow I still feel blue
Even though my wish came true
I feel some day we shall have to end
But pleassssse let's still be friends.

Tyffany Booker (12)
The Angmering School

Freedom!

The door is wide open
They've left it ajar
I could sneak down the garden
As far as the car.

My whiskers are twitching,
My nose sniffs the air.
The lure of the garden
Will always be there.

I make a quick dash,
As far as the tree.
At last I've escaped
And now I'm free.

I rush to the pavement
Then wait till it's clear,
Cross over the road,
Without any fear.

I head for the park
With one flick of my tail,
The escape from my prison
Will surely not fail.

Oh no what's that?
I heard a loud sound.
It's coming right for me
It's a big, barking hound.

I'll run for my life
Back to my home,
I learned my lesson
No more shall I roam!

Keri Dawson (12)
The Angmering School

The Stalking Cats

The cat, its eyes sparkling like gems
In the darkness of the night.
Slowly fixing its prey
Stalking through the grass
Waiting for a fight.

Suddenly, wails like babies fill the air,
They hiss and spit at each other.
Motionless like statues with arched backs
To watch them makes you shudder.

They pounce - claws outstretched
And roll like a twisting snake.
Then one gives up - he's had enough
Like lightning he bolts the gate!

Zeba Ghorishi (11)
The Angmering School

My Poem

Before
I love my mum, I love my dad
But when he left I felt empty and sad,
Floods of tears fell down my face
As it feels like I've hit a hard base.
I cried and cried all night long
I didn't stop until the dawn.

After
A couple of years have passed without my dad,
And after all, it wasn't that bad.
I had my mum to look after me,
I didn't understand, I didn't see
I will see my dad about twice a year,
But he lives far away, he doesn't live near.

Abigail Allen (13)
The Angmering School

Cats In The Cornfield

Kittens are playing in the cornfield,
Mother's hunting for food,
Father's lazing in the sun
Auntie's in a mood.

Nan is acting cool,
Gramps is up a tree, chasing a bird,
Kittens chasing a piece of wool,
Uncle's playing football.

Now it's getting dark,
It's time for tea.
Kittens are in bed already
Mum and Dad are tired,
Gran and Gramps are out.
Mum and Dad are going to bed
So now it's time for lights out.

Lucy Darling & Jodie Carter (11)
The Angmering School

Netball

I like to play netball
'Cause it's my best ball
My position is goal attack
I'll never give it back
I like to score
And love scoring more
When we work as a team
We seem to treat them mean
I aim my shots
And hope to score lots
I've played since I was seven
And now I'm eleven
That's four years of netball
I'm still thinking it's my best ball.

Paris Osborne (11)
The Angmering School

Battle Is Nothing

The death of a soldier is the start of hatred,
And hatred is the start of a battle.
For neither can claim right as both are equals.
Both teams are human
Both teams scared
Both teams alive at first
And dead at the end.

One man is nothing to a leader
But everything to a family.
No leader has been correct
And no leader will be when there are still battles.

The only good life is a battle-free life where death is not seen.
When a gun is fired, the sinister figure is there.
Chasing the bullet, hoping that it gives the creature a meal.
Although you cannot see it, you can feel it,
And sense it.
When a battle starts, the creature comes out of its lair
Every time a victim is killed, the creature lives for another day.

The black figure has no shape
For the only thing stopping it growing, is peace.
Although when peace hides, death thrives
And for every person who wants peace,
There is another who would deny it.
Yet the strength of peace could grow
And in its growth would mean a day less with the beast of death.

No leader in the world wants to relinquish its power,
And until they do, the sinister beast of death
Will always have a meal.

Stuart Loxton (11)
The Angmering School

The Match

The crowd go wild, they're cheering loud and clear,
The players hear the deafening row,
Most of them have no fear.
The coach speaks gently, time for team talk
in the dressing room.
One of the players, staring blankly, eyes full
of doom and gloom.

The team jog out of the tunnel,
Keen and raring to go!
Blood is pumping and adrenaline is flowing,
More pre-match nerves are beginning to show.
The ref looks at his watch, the teams are ready.
He blows the whistle for the match to start,
The player from each side attack,
A goalkeeper dives, makes a great save and shows great heart.

Whistle blown, it's half-time now,
All players look worn out.
Coach thinks it's a disaster, no goals have been scored,
He yells and screams and shouts.
Half-time talk is over, heads held high,
The players look much stronger.
Back on the pitch, only second half to go,
Could they go on much longer?

Ninety minutes have been played and it's one a piece.
Who played the best? Who should have scored
one more goal at least?
The match is over, the crowd are quiet,
Moving slowly they disappear.
The disappointed coach cannot believe his luck,
He shrugs his shoulders and sheds a tear.

Dean Cronk (11)
The Angmering School

The Sea

The waves crashed against the rocks
And sped up the shore,
The white horses ran back,
As the people gazed in awe.

The aquatic fire burned,
Waves flew into the sky,
The fisherman's boat fought,
But was gone in a blink of an eye.

The news crews arrived
And filled the sea with hate,
It came up behind them so quiet,
It dragged them down and felt it had ate.

Everybody trembled,
They trembled with fear,
The sea was now approaching,
That was all they could hear.

Thomas Trencher (11)
The Angmering School

Autumn And Winter

The sun is shining low,
With a glittery autumn glow.
It will not be too long,
Till the first of winter's snow.

The clouds are thick and grey,
Indoors we have to stay,
It now seems too long,
Till the warmth of a summer's day.

Ellie Pocock (11)
The Angmering School

I Was Born Into A Silent World

Now I can hear . . .
The bark of my puppy
The purring of a cat
The tune of a bird on a happy day
The spoon dropping in a bowl
The crunching of the flakes
The spreading of peanut butter
The scraping noise it makes

The sizzling of the frying pan
The ticking of the gas grill
The bubbling of the bath
As it starts to fill
The gurgle of the water down the plughole

The pitter-patter of the rain on the window
When I wash up I hear the hollow noise of the water
In the pans
The crashing of the pans in the cupboard

The crying of the baby
The shouts of my sister
The creaking of the stair
And the floorboards as I tiptoe

I was born into the world of silence.
Life is full of noises
Every day I learn a new sound
Life will never be the same.

Laurie Talbot (11)
The Angmering School

Loneliness

It is torture,
Day after day the element of friends in your life,
They just never seem to come,
The isolation, the fear,
He is overwhelmed by dreaded pain.

Inside the room, there lies a boy,
A fickle boy, a healthy boy,
A boy who has no friends,
Upon his door it reads:
Enter at your own peril!

An odd sensation for such a child,
He lies alone, quivering at night,
His soul seems to snap in half,
It occurs to him more than ever before,
He is a failure.

This sudden possibility strikes him like a baseball bat,
He feels nausea; he has to lie down,
He considers it,
No he has now a rejection towards it,
How to decipher the truth?

As far as he is concerned each day can rain,
The mortal darkness falls not irregular to him,
His only friends are his parents,
Although they are not aware of such an occurring,
He dreads the next day, he hopes that he doesn't awake.

Andrew Follows (11)
The Angmering School

Fierce Friend

Amber eyes peering through the leaves,
Camouflage stripes behind the trees,
Sharp white fangs waiting for prey,
Out bounces a kitten ready to play.

Sara Trott (11)
The Angmering School

My Sister Maisy!

On the 9th of June this year,
My mum was not here.
Why? She was having a baby,
My little sister Maisy!

She was really, really small,
Only 50cm tall!
I'm ever so happy and proud,
If only her screams weren't so loud!

She is so cute and lovely,
Her dribble's very bubbly!
She giggles when I'm funny,
She laughs when I tickle her tummy!

Her name is Maisy West,
She really is the best!
She's the new member of my family,
And I'm so very, very *happy!*

Hope Blandamer (12)
The Angmering School

Top Shot

Keeping their eye on the ball,
Erupting the anger with good play,
Stampeding to the goal,
Man U take a shot and I begin to yell, '1-0!'
Half-time psyching up again,
Arsenal take a shot and miss all the way.

The crowd gets cheery and ruthless
It comes to an end,
Also they're half way round the bend.
Man U get excited and play with the crowd.
It comes to the end,
'Very happy result,' I shout aloud.

Harriet Hislop (11)
The Angmering School

The England Football Team

The summer season's over,
Autumn's just begun,
The football season's started
And England have just won.
The first game is coming,
They're gonna be alive,
Owen makes a run for the goal
And Heskey makes it five!

At half-time they're 6-5 down
They going down a hole
Rooney wins a penalty,
Beckham's gonna take,
Yes it's in the goal!
They're drawing with the Germans,
They're gonna have to win,
Scholesy has the header,
Yes it's in again!

Sophie Anning (12)
The Angmering School

Fire

November the 5th is Bonfire Night,
Chill in the air, coats to keep warm,
Dad with a match sets it alight,
All around the fire in a big swarm.

Standing there watching the fire,
Flames of yellow, orange and red,
With smoke drifting higher and higher,
But some clouds are gathering overhead.

The fire now is starting to die out,
Go indoors and snuggle down tight.
All the children start to shout,
'Let's go to sleep it's nearly midnight.'

Kirstie Torode (11)
The Angmering School

The Green Van

I hate, I hate,
my uncle's van.
It doesn't even
have a fan.
It's got millions of dents,
from diving into a fence.
It runs like mad
and thinks I'm glad.
The seat smells of cheese,
under my knees.
It's fortunate it
drove into the sea.

Robbie Maynard (11)
The Angmering School

The Wind

The wind it is here, it is there
It is everywhere
It is in the leaves
It is in the trees
They have voices when the wind is there
We hear the wind
We see the wind
We know when it's there
But our eyes deceive us
The wind . . .
Our invisible friend.

Matt West (11)
The Angmering School

Winter

Winter,
The cold laugh,
The bitter cry,
The howls,
The pain,
Whispers.

Blowing against me,
The wind lashing,
Trees have fallen down,
Thunder and lightning,
Horror-struck children,
The pain,
The grief,
The shock.

Hear my cries,
Hear my howls,
Help me now.

Jade Bearham (12)
The Angmering School

Basketball

Basketball is a well good sport
Showing off skill up and down the court
Shooting some hoops
Doing alleyoops
Watching the Lakers on NBA
Better than us 'cause we can't play
Michael Jordan, simply the best
Better than Kobe and the rest
Taking some shots from the 3 pointer mark
Watch that ball soaring like a dart
Some of the players are really tall
To stop high shots with the ball.

Matt Roberts (11)
The Angmering School

Animals

Animals are big
Animals are small
Animals are fat
And animals are tall

Elephants are fat
Giraffes are mighty tall
Tigers linger in the middle
Mice are really small

Animals can be kept as pets
Dolphins and tigers too
Monkeys, zebras and most other animals
Can be adopted too

Animals, animals, big and small
Animals, animals, cute and tall
Animals, animals, I love animals
Animals, animals, don't we all.

Laura Allen (11)
The Angmering School

A Poem About Football

Going down the park at half-past two, just me and my ball.
Smacking it in the back of the net,
When along came a man,
Who said, 'Show me what you've got.'
Before I knew it I was a millionaire
Playing in London at The Lane.
Playing all day can be a bit of a pain.
Then all my dreams all came true
Playing United in the cup
Scored the winning goal in a 3-2 thump
I was the star of the world
Everyone loved me I was king with a crown.
Everyone happy under the sun and already got a house in Hawaii.

Harry Standing (11)
The Angmering School

I Suck At Poems

For some people it comes easily
The rhyming words just flow
But for me it's the other way round
Because my brain just doesn't grow.

Some people like to perform their work
But I couldn't care
I suck at poems because
I just don't have that writing flair.

Jasmine Smith (11)
The Angmering School

Good Days

Fridays, Fridays, I love Fridays
'Cause it's the end of the week, yippee!
Fridays, Fridays are so good,
So everybody come and play.
They make me bubble like a bubbly bath
'Cause I can pop and jump like a bubble and bounce.
Just the word Friday makes me glad
That's the end of my glad poem.

Naomi Horn (11)
The Angmering School

Hunting Tiger

Tiger's on the plain,
hunting easy game,
he hides and takes his pick,
and leaps ever so quick.
The herd run away,
as the tiger eats the catch of the day.

Sam McCarthy (11)
The Angmering School

Hair

Hair is long
hair is short
some are hairy
some are not.
Hair is coloured
hair is plain
some are scary
some are not.
Hair is curly
hair is straight
some wear wigs
some do not.
Hair is on faces
hair is on hands
some are spiky
some are not.
Hair runs away from you when you're old.
I like hair cos it's always there.

Ryan Tester (11)
The Angmering School

Terrifying Spiders

If you don't do your homework
the spiders will come
spiders creeping
spiders crawling
spiders hanging from behind
spiders leaping from tree to tree
spiders' long and spindly legs
spiders jumping on your head.
Open your mouth and begin to
scream.

Robert Bishop (11)
The Angmering School

Birth And Death

A mother is crying
There is blood all around,
Some on the ceiling
Some on the ground.
She is relieved
The battle is done -
No it's not a war! She's just had a son.

A woman is crying
There is blood all around,
Some on the ceiling
Some on the ground.
She is relieved that her life is done,
This is suicide -
She has just lost her son.

His life was cut short because a bomb fell on him
No bomb fell on her.
But now she is dead as well.
One minute he was there and the next
He was gone!
Somewhere in the world
Something's gone wrong!

Lucy Sambrook (13)
The Angmering School

Night Hunter

The creature of the night,
The one with blood-tipped teeth,
The murderous fiend without a soul,
The one who's seen beneath.

He shares the devil's spirit,
He has the witch fire eyes,
He deals in O's and A's,
And countless dirty lies.

Some say he drinks for pleasure,
Some say he drinks to live,
Some say he should have been killed long ago,
But death's not theirs to give.

He died when he was buried,
To forever avoid the sun,
That fateful day, July 14th,
His vampire life begun.

No one shed a tear for him,
For no one knew his name,
To the gods and fates up in the heavens,
His life was just a game.

No one shed a tear for him,
And no one ever will
His life on Earth now means three things,
To hunt, to feed, to kill.

It's not his fault what he's become,
He did not choose his fate,
He cannot control what he does,
So don't stay out too late . . .

Charlotte Turner (11)
The Angmering School